Fighters of the Sky

Fighters of the Sky

Accounts of the Air War over France by
American Pilots

Night Bombing with the Bedouins
Robert H. Reece

With Three Accounts from 'New England Aviators
1914-1918'

A Happy Warrior
William Muir Russel

LEONAUR

Fighters of the Sky
Accounts of the Air War over France by American Pilots
Night Bombing with the Bedouins
by Robert H. Reece
With Three Accounts from 'New England Aviators 1914-1918'
A Happy Warrior
by William Muir Russel

FIRST EDITION

First published under the titles
Night Bombing with the Bedouins
and
A Happy Warrior

Leonaur is an imprint of Oakpast Ltd

ISBN: 978-1-78282-553-1 (hardcover)
ISBN: 978-1-78282-554-8 (softcover)

http://www.leonaur.com

Publisher's Notes

The views expressed in this book are not necessarily
those of the publisher.

Contents

Night Bombing with the Bedouins

LIEUTENANT ROBERT H. REECE

Contents

Dedication

IN A SPIRIT OF THE DEEPEST REVERENCE I DEDICATE THIS UNWORTHY EFFORT TO THE MEMORY OF A TRUE SPORTSMAN, A LOYAL FRIEND, AND A GALLANT OFFICER WHO WAS KILLED IN ACTION WHILE SERVING HIS COUNTRY AS A PILOT IN THE AMERICAN AIR SERVICE,

LIEUTENANT SAMUEL PIERCE MANDELL

AMERICA HAS GIVEN OF THE FINEST OF HER YOUTH TO UPHOLD THE CAUSE OF RIGHT, BUT SHE HAS GIVEN NO ONE OF MORE SPLENDID PROMISE THAN HE, WHOSE SERVICE WAS AN EXAMPLE OF DEVOTION TO DUTY, OF READINESS FOR ACTION, AND OF UNDAUNTED COURAGE.

HIS LIFE WAS AN INSPIRATION TO THE LIVING "TO CARRY ON" AND FINISH THE GREAT STRUGGLE FOR WHICH HE DIED, THAT HE AND THOSE LIKE HIM MAY NOT HAVE DIED IN VAIN.

CHAPTER 1

Per Ardua Ad Astra

In prehistoric times the first man to make for himself a stone hatchet probably became the greatest warrior of his particular region. He may not have been as strong physically as his neighbour, but with the aid of so marvellous an invention as a stone hatchet he undoubtedly conquered his enemies and became a great prehistoric potentate, until some other great man made a larger and stronger hatchet; so down to the present invention has followed invention and improvement has been added to improvement to such an extent that it is difficult to imagine what new weapon of destruction man can develop in the future.

What would the past generation have said of a man who had prophesied great armies fighting in the air? Even in the early months of the war there were but few who realized what an important part of the war was to be carried on in the newly conquered element. When the infantry saw an occasional box-kite-looking machine drifting slowly over the lines, struggling to keep itself aloft, how many, I wonder, foresaw that in a few months these machines would be swooping down on them like swallows, raking them with machine guns by day and bombing them by night? How many artillery officers laughed at the suggestion that a day was coming when thousands of great guns would be directed from the air? Yet in a few short months two great blind fighting giants, their arms stretching from the Belgian coast to the Swiss border, learned to see each other; and their eyes were in the air.

The first aeroplanes to cross the lines carried no armament; they were for reconnaissance work only; they would fly a few miles back of the enemy lines, have a good look around, and then come back and report what they had seen. Often British and German machines would pass quite close to each other. Flying was considered sufficiently dangerous, not to add a further danger to it by attacking enemy machines.

The Germans, however, because they greatly outnumbered the British in the air, had more eyes to see with; something had to be done; so rifles were carried by the British and a finer sport than shooting ducks came into vogue. This quickly led to the carrying of machine guns. Ingenuity in devising sights to compensate for the speed of our own machines and to gauge a proper deflection according to the speed and angle of approach of the enemy machine, soon decreased the advantage the enemy aviators had through superior numbers.

For example, if our machine was flying at the rate of one hundred miles per hour and the enemy's machine was travelling past us in the opposite direction at an equal rate, our fore-sight nullified our motion and enabled us to shoot as if from a stationary base, while our back-sight helped us to gauge that imaginary point at which to shoot where our bullets and the enemy machine would meet. In other words, we shot at an enemy machine although we ourselves were travelling rapidly, exactly as a sportsman shoots at a bird on the wing.

Then a new aeroplane was developed, the single-seater tractor, with a Vickers gun, synchronized to shoot through the rapidly revolving propeller so as to avoid the blades. These machines were used to patrol the lines and keep enemy machines from crossing, or to accompany a reconnaissance machine as protector; for they were very much faster, easier to manoeuvre, and altogether very much more efficient fighters. At first they operated singly, but it was soon discovered that two of these scout machines operating together invariably obtained better success than when operating alone. This led to formation flying, and up to the cessation of hostilities these formations grew in size and varied in shape.

The reconnaissance work was soon divided into classes: long and short reconnaissance and photographic reconnaissance. The long reconnaissance dealt with enemy movements far behind the lines; the short reconnaissance with enemy activities near the front. The photographic reconnaissance consisted of taking aerial photographs of everything of military importance within flying radius. These photographs pieced together showed the enemy defences along the entire British front and their changes from day to day.

Wireless apparatus was soon attached to aeroplanes, and this enabled an aviator to communicate with people on the ground many miles away; and so what was called artillery observation was developed. Roughly speaking, this is the direction of the fire of our batteries against enemy targets; but, just as specialization came in reconnaissance and fighting, so now machines specialized in artillery observation. Today, (1919), the efficiency of the artillery depends largely upon its direction from the air. For instance, when a battery takes over a new area the gunners may be called upon to fire at certain targets, such as cross-roads or houses used as infantry headquarters or ammunition and stores dumps, at a moment's notice. Consequently, if these targets are registered by aeroplane, all the gunners have to do when called upon to open fire is to refer to their registration book which will give them the necessary angles to use on their sights, then, by allowing for the temperature of the day and the direction and velocity of the wind, their shooting is certain to be far more accurate than it would be if the target had not been previously registered. The registration of targets today without the use of aeroplanes is very often impossible.

The registration of targets from the air, however, is not the most important part of this work. For instance, a machine will be flying over enemy territory; the observer will see the flash of an enemy gun and will pin-point its position on his map, which is marked off into large and small lettered and numbered squares. This operation enables him to send by wireless what is known as a zone call, giving the exact location of the enemy battery to all of our batteries within range. The enemy battery then has to move suddenly, if it is ever to move at all.

Barrages can also be controlled very efficiently from the air, so, considering the comparatively short time that aeroplanes have been used in this work and the wonderful results that have been obtained, it does not take much imagination to see the necessity for all future artillery officers to be trained as aviators.

In the earlier stages of the war it was very difficult for Headquarters to keep in close touch with the infantry during a "push"; consequently, considerable loss of life might result from one portion of the line advancing out of contact with another. Probably the eagerness of raw troops to keep on advancing regardless of their objective has led to a considerable and unnecessary loss of life. The aeroplane can be used in these situations to great advantage, and after the development of what is known as "contact patrol" the aeroplane became the connecting link between Headquarters and the infantry.

It was not until 1916 that the full powers of the aeroplane as an offensive weapon began to be realized. Bombing was done, but it was of a desultory nature, and although the number of machines engaged in this work steadily increased, and the work itself became more and more diversified and specialized, it was not until 1918 that the possibilities of the aeroplane as a purely offensive weapon were appreciated.

An aeroplane can operate far back of the enemy lines, both in the day and at night; enemy troops in transport can be bombed: railway stations, sidings, etc., damaged; transports of all kinds delayed; and ammunition dumps, when located, can be blown up. In fact, military targets of all sorts can be attacked from the air that cannot be reached in any other way. The very foundation of a nation's strength in war, its industry, can be attacked from the air and, if attacked on a large enough scale, can be destroyed. For instance, eighty *per cent* of the German steel industry was within bombing range of the Allies. The Westphalian group of high-grade steel industries centred at Essen is about two hundred miles from Nancy. If this group had been bombed on a large scale the source of supply of German guns and munitions could have been destroyed; for a blast furnace destroyed cannot be replaced within nine months, and the destruction of the central electrical plant of a steel factory would place the entire factory out of operation for at least six months. The hundreds of bombing machines which the English aeroplane factories were turning out at the time hostilities ceased, and the thousands of men being trained for bombing, make one wonder what would have happened to the German industries if the war had continued through the spring of 1919.

Besides these hundreds of aeroplanes under construction and the thousands of men in training, the Royal Air Force had in operation, November 11, 1918, over twenty thousand aeroplanes, over thirty thousand aviators, and over two hundred thousand mechanics and other personnel.

CHAPTER 2

The "Bedouin" Squadron

The "Bedouin" Squadron, so called because as a unit it was constantly moved from place to place, and because its members as individuals were wanderers at heart, was formed in September, 1917, equipped with the large Handley-Page bombing planes, and sent to the Nancy front to carry out pioneer work in long-distance bombing. The "Bedouins," as the officers of this squadron were called, first saw the light of day in England, Scotland, Ireland, America, India, Canada, South Africa, and Australia. Before becoming aviators many of them had fought in the infantry on the western front, in Gallipoli, and in Egypt; some as officers, some as privates, but for no general reason, unless the law of nature which prevents squirrels from remaining on the ground also applies to men, they one by one in divers ways drifted into the Flying Corps, and flew different types of machines on different fronts until brought together and formed, "willy-nilly," into the Bedouin Squadron.

1

There was "Jimmie," whose insides had been shot away in Gallipoli. He was the envy of the officers' mess, because his newly acquired digestive apparatus, composed principally of silver tubes, could assimilate more wine without producing ill results than any other five members of the mess. Jimmie was not a flying officer; by all the laws of nature he should have been a corpse, but he had a heart which disregarded an intestine designed by a surgeon who must have been a plumber in some previous incarnation, and this great heart carried him through four years of war, and made of him an energising force to all who came in contact with him. It was not until after the cessation of hostilities that the soul of this hero was liberated from the poor

17

JIMMIE WALKS UP AND DOWN THE TRENCH

maimed body with its mechanical digestive system.

Jimmie was the First Lieutenant of the Station; it was his job to see to the discipline of the two hundred and fifty mechanics, riggers, carpenters, armorers, drivers, and officers' stewards. He did this in such a way as to make all the men love him except the few, very few, who were surly slackers, and these feared him worse than death itself. Jimmie was always just, but he demanded results. To those who shirked he was a just judge and an unsympathetic jury; so, under Jimmie, slackers soon became demons for work, and later on learned like the others to love him. To those who produced results, he was a father.

I remember that shortly after the squadron took up its residence on the Nancy front, the Huns came over and bombed us severely; many of the mechanics were fresh from the factories in England and were quite unaccustomed to seeing the damage that one hundred pounds of high explosive can do to the delicate anatomy of the human being; panic seized them; but a greater fear possessed them when Jimmie's orders burst upon them like the *rat-tat-tat* of a machine gun; they marched as if on parade into the trenches, recently dug behind the hangars; then Jimmie, smoking an occasional cigarette, strolled up and down in front during the three hours' bombardment.

So the men soon learned, under Jimmie, the value of discipline; it meant their safety when under fire, and it meant freedom from military punishments. They were quick to grasp the fact that any negligence on their part might mean death to the aviator who flew in the neglected aeroplane. Flagrant neglect they soon learned might cause other deaths than those suffered by the unfortunate aviators.

2

There was Sammie, a prototype of the caricatured Englishman in our comic papers. Every American theatre-goer has seen Sammie exaggerated on the music-hall stage.

Sammie was a small boy with an eyebrow on his upper lip and an apparently permanent window over his right eye. Before joining the Flying Corps, he had served seventeen months in the trenches as a private; finally, driven mad with filth, rats, and other vermin, he captured an enemy machine-gun emplacement single-handed, and was given a commission. Shortly afterwards he joined the Flying Corps, probably because he could not keep his new uniform clean while in the trenches.

Sammie was always immaculate, and as a uniform gives one very little opportunity to express one's individuality in dress, Sammie carried his handkerchief up his sleeve. Even Generals envied Sammie's field boots and everyone who met him wanted to know the name of his tailor.

In peace-time Sammie would have looked like a toy Pom with a ribbon around its neck; but a more imperturbable man in the face of danger never lived.

"My word" was the expression used by Sammie to denote every degree of human emotion. If it was Sammie's lot to draw the occasional egg served in the Bedouin mess, his only remark when it hopped out of reach would be, "My word."

I remember one night when both of our machines were out of action, Sammie and I, who slept in the same hut, went to bed at the early hour of twelve o'clock; at about one in the morning the Huns dropped their first bomb very close to us; a picture of Sammie's mother was on a stand beside the head of his cot; a fragment of the bomb came through the wall of the hut and shattered this picture; I landed, as far as I know involuntarily, in the middle of the floor with a lighted torch in my hand; Sammie saw the shattered remains of his mother's picture; "My word, mother will be pleased," he said, turned over and was sound asleep instantly. I know Sammie slept because he never remarked on my taking a short cut to the trenches through the window.

Another time when a Hun bomb dropped in the officers' trench and failed to explode, Sammie, who was but two feet away, tried to lift it, failed, and then lay full length upon it, believing it to be of the "delay action" variety; when our major, a bomb expert, appeared on the scene a few moments later and laughingly declared the bomb a "dud," Sammie's embarrassment expressed itself in "My word." If the detonating apparatus of this bomb had been all that the Huns intended it to be, Sammie would have returned to minute specks of dust and his name would have been added to the long list of dead heroes; but since the bomb was a "dud," Sammie was made the butt of his friends' wit.

Sammie was always philosophical. He was once ordered to take a new machine on a very long raid. We had all examined this new aeroplane and declared it a "dud"; so we cheered Sammie up as well as we could by drinking his health and inquiring into his taste in flowers. Undismayed, Sammie took the machine off the ground, with the wheel held into his stomach; the rigging of the machine was such that it would fly on an even plane longitudinally if the wheel was kept back as far as possible. By all the laws of aeronautics this aeroplane should have crashed before leaving the ground, but it did not. Sammie climbed it to five hundred feet in an hour and a half. As Sammie now had seven and one half hours' petrol left and was still four hours away from his objective, it would have been quite justifiable for him to return without going any farther; in fact, it was the only reasonable thing for him to do; but Sammie always trusted to luck rather than reason, and his luck did not fail him.

One engine "conked" and he was forced to turn back. He fired his forced landing signal when approaching the aerodrome, but the aerodrome was being bombed by the Huns in a very thorough manner and Sammie had to land in complete darkness, the inevitable result being a crash. Sammie extricated himself from the wreckage, found that both of his companions were dead, rescued one of the machine guns from its damaged mounting, together with several drums of ammunition and practised his marksmanship on the enemy planes until an enemy bomb ruined his clothes and left him, after a few months in the hospital, minus an arm.

3

There was "Jock," a "wee bonnie laddie," from the south of Scotland. He stood five feet three inches tall when wearing field boots with exceptionally high heels, but that did not prevent him from braining a Hun with the Hun's own wrench some sixty miles back of the enemy's front lines, and this is how it happened.

One morning, about three o'clock, information arrived, together with a complete and undamaged Hun aeroplane and two friendly Hun aviators, that at a certain German switch station a troop train and an ammunition train were due to pass at a certain hour. Jock and his pal left the congenial beer barrel, turned the friendly Hun aviators over to the guard, made themselves acquainted with the Hun aeroplane, refilled it with petrol and oil, and departed on a merry adventure. Forgetting that the Hun machine would be subject to attack by our own aviators, Jock and his companion were in a great dilemma when so attacked.

Of course, they could not protect themselves by a counter-fire, but when a man is born in Scotland, and is a direct descendant of oatmeal-eating bandits, he naturally has a keener brain than even the Jews can boast of; consequently, by spinning nose dives and other signs of lack of control the wily Scot gleefully gained the enemy's side of the lines. Here he was unmolested, although Hun aviators must have been astonished to see one of their own machines engaged in the

British sport of "hedge-hopping"; *i.e.*, flying close to the ground and "zooming" up over trees, houses, etc.

In due time Jock and his companion landed in a small field a few hundred yards away from the all-important switch station. Here they descended and under pretence of examining their engine, although the first one of the ever-curious crowd was still several fields away, they looked up the word "wrench" in an English-German pocket dictionary; they then marched off to the switch station. Fortunately there was but one occupant, for neither Jock nor his companion could talk German, and the idiocy of not carrying a more serviceable weapon than a pocket dictionary never occurred to the mad Scot until his companion began to make weird gurgling sounds, evidently intended for the language of the Hun, addressed to the astonished station-master.

Then down through generations of oatmeal-eating bandits came a glimmer of sense to Jock. He grabbed the first thing within reach, a wrench, and brained the Hun station-master with a blow; then the mad but somewhat sobered adventurers found and pulled the switch lever so as to bring the approaching trains into collision, and departed. When Jock saw the crowd which had collected about his aeroplane, he took a solemn oath never to touch beer but to stick to whiskey; but the crowd, which included a few Hun soldiers, respectfully made way for the "camouflaged" British aviators and a few moments later, wet with cold perspiration, they were in the air. Thoroughly sobered, they made for home with their engine "full out." Six weeks later "intelligence" reported that a German troop train and ammunition train had collided.

4

There was "Mac," a North of England man. Before the war he was a typical English sportsman; he lived for hunting, and polo was his hobby. Like the rest of his class he pushed his way into the fighting line as soon as possible, as a private in the First Hundred Thousand. But eventually his genius expressed itself and leaving the known walks of man he became a master of the newly conquered element. Mac's mind was not limited by science, his soul was not dwarfed by religious prejudice, he held no political position, and he had no personal military ambition. He fought to defeat a threat to the civilization he believed in, to preserve a form of government that his ancestors had bled and died for, and to secure a future for his tiny son free from the hell of war. Mac, like every other man who had the courage to fight, and if necessary, die for his beliefs, hoped that the fighting man would be allowed to fight on until these ends had been achieved so that those who had died should not have made the great sacrifice in vain.

He hoped, like all other fighting men, that politicians would not be given the power to render valueless to posterity the sacrifice of hundreds of thousands of lives; but Mac was merely a man, of fearless integrity, honesty of purpose, with humanitarian ideals, and a believer in Democracy; he could not realize that a large majority, because of selfishness, ignorance, and a lack of the spirit of self-sacrifice, do not deserve the right to vote. But Mac was a sportsman and a gentle-man, the descendant of generations of men who faced death willingly in a cause they knew was honourable and who died happily in the thought that their death made life easier for future generations. So Mac did not worry about the selfish ambitions of men; he did all he could to win the World War.

I first met Mac a few months after he flew a Handley-Page ma-chine from London to Constantinople and back to Salonica, a distance of over two thousand miles. Mac was a captain then, he is a captain now, but no living man has done more damage to the Hun than Mac has done. A far greater leader of men than his great uncle, who was a general in our Civil War, Mac gave a soul to the Bedouin Squadron. To Mac's leadership is due the first bombings of Mannheim, Coblenz, Thionville, Frankfort, and Cologne.

It was Mac who flew a German aeroplane to Sedan, followed a "spotted" train to a nearby station, swooped down as the German High Command left the train and opened on them with his machine gun. It was Mac who landed over ten times near Karlsruhe at night and returned with invaluable information. But it is not because of the innumerable suicidal adventures of which Mac is the hero that every Bedouin, no matter in what part of the world he may be, always drinks a silent toast to Mac whenever possible; it is because every Bedouin realizes that a great man carried out a small man's job in a great way.

5

"Gus" was the president of the Bedouin mess, and probably because of an early education at Heidelberg, he believed in starving the Brit-ish aviator. At all events, while Gus was mess president we all starved with agonizing slowness, for Gus had but two ideas of what consti-tuted a menu. Our meals consisted solely of "bully beef" and Brussels sprouts; this meal was varied occasionally by leaving out the sprouts. To every indignant complaint from long-suffering members of the officers' mess, Gus would answer with the incontrovertible statement that "humming-birds' tongues cannot be purchased with tuppence"; this incontrovertible statement always reduced the complaining member to frothings at the mouth and other signs of inexpressible rage.

Nevertheless, under the starvation system of Gus's stewardship a large credit balance was established at the *Société Générale*, which enabled the succeeding mess president to replace the expert electrician, who by army wisdom had been converted into a poisonous cook, with a Frenchman, whose cooking was not cooking at all, but an art which filled the Bedouins with admiration and destroyed their waist lines. Six-course banquets, ending with a rare old yellow Chartreuse, became the order of the day, and whenever some seductive delicacy defied analysis we would ask Gus if it contained the tongue of the humming-bird.

But Gus, although a failure in always satisfying the epicurean tastes of the Bedouins, won fame by being the first to bomb Cologne.

6

"Mid" was a Yank who joined the squadron a few months before its "bust-up." Mid had been a private in the first American contingent to arrive in France; but because he was born in Cleveland, Ohio, and knew that automobiles were manufactured in Detroit, Michigan, he was given a commission. The Bedouins first met Mid in January, 1918. He had run his car—Mid was always driving a car—into a snowdrift, and wandered a couple of miles through a blizzard in search of help. Fortunately for us, he tumbled into our mess in the midst of a "storm celebration"; *i.e.*, a celebration in honour of a storm which forces birds and all other inhabitants of the air to seek shelter. Mid was pounced upon, placed in front of the fire, and given hot rum. A crew of men were sent off to dig his "benzine buggy" out of the snow and convey it to Mid's station, it having been decided that Mid should spend the night with the Bedouins.

Mid soon won the hearts of the Bedouins by showing a proper appreciation for hot rum, and when he prefaced his first remark to the C.O. with "Say, kid," the Bedouins realized that Mid gave every promise of making this "storm celebration" unique in Bedouin history, and as far as Mid was concerned it certainly was.

Mid entered into the spirit of the occasion with Western thoroughness and learned a lesson in a few hours which it has taken some men years to learn—that hot rum when taken on a cold and empty stomach must be treated with respect; in fact, a certain amount of coyness is not out of place. Mid was soon being supported on a chair while he delivered an epic on the "soul of a jellyfish"; he was then tossed in the "sacred blanket" and put through other Bedouin initiations; after which he was tucked comfortably in Jock's bed, while Jock, bound hand and foot and rolled in blankets, made horrid Highland remarks from the draughty floor of the hut.

Dear old Mid, however, bore no ill-will to the Bedouins for what he might have considered unceremonious treatment of an American officer who was an honoured guest. The next morning with a humble but dignified mien, Mid apologized for everything that he had done. As a matter of fact, the only disreputable thing Mid had done while under the influence of an excess of hot rum on an empty stomach was to make friends with a few men whom the Huns had sworn to kill on sight.

Nothing daunted, Mid soon "wangled" permission to become attached to the Bedouin Squadron, and a more dare-devil spirit and lovable comrade than Mid did not exist among the Bedouins. He was always as keen for work as he was "full out" for a party, and he was always the life of a celebration. I remember one night when the C.O. read out at dinner a telegram which concisely stated that His Majesty the King had awarded to one of the Bedouins a very great honour, Mid broke loose. "Say, kids," he said, "I want to say right here that it's a great honour for my mother's younger son to be a Bedouin, and since it's a 'dud' night I want to ask your permission, Sir" (turning to the C.O.), "to present every Bedouin with a quart of the best." Permission being given by the C.O. on the condition that the C.O. himself would be allowed to share in the "largess," every Bedouin had placed before him a quart of Heidsieck Monopole. Songs and speeches followed, and Mid, since he could not "take the air," took the floor.

"Fellow citizens," he said, balancing himself on an upturned beer barrel, "it gives me great pleasure to be able to stand before you this evening"; support given and applause. "It has always seemed to me that the greatest country in the world might be considered a bit slow in entering the war." (Hear! Hear!) "But, gentlemen, now that we are in, I want to say that we will be the first out." (Loud applause!) "I want you to understand that because the United States has always been considered the historic enemy of Great Britain, Germany was enabled to persuade an ignorant electorate that the United States and Germany were friends. But now we are in, we are in to the finish. When I say finish, gentlemen, I mean a finish to the fighting, but I beg of you to be careful of the non-fighting part of my country's population, and their representatives. More I cannot say, except this, if ever your king or your sea-power is threatened, you may depend upon every true American; we owe you a debt, and depend upon it every descendant of the founders of our country will die before that obligation is allowed to be repudiated." With loud cheers, Mid was lifted from his perch.

7

The Bedouin who held the unenvied record for crashes was known throughout the service as "Killem." Almost every time he went on a raid he crashed his machine, fortunately for him on this side of the lines. One night, returning from a raid on the Boche magneto works at Stuttgart, he lost his way and was forced to land, because of engine trouble, in France, near the Swiss border. The topography of the country here being mountainous, he was fortunate in merely "writing off" his aeroplane. He might easily have killed himself and his two companions, but he came out of the crash quite unhurt except for a severe chill contracted by a forced sojourn in the icy waters of a shallow pond. Pinned beneath the wreckage of his machine with an unpleasant ripple of water in close proximity to his chin, Killem had an excellent opportunity to think over his past sins while his companions in misery, who had been thrown clear for no other reason apparently except that the devil takes care of his own, struggled manfully, one with a broken arm and the other with a wrenched knee, to release him from the pressure of wreckage which held him helpless.

A few nights after this unpleasant experience the mad fellow "took off" down wind. This idiotic method of leaving the ground resulted in his being barely able to rise above the roofs of the near-by village and brought him into direct contact with the church spire. The spire being of solid construction withstood the impact; the aeroplane did not. So Killem and his companions, together with the wrecked Handley-Page and one thousand five hundred and sixty-eight pounds of undetonated bombs descended onto the street below—*UNDETONATED.* It was exceedingly fortunate for the inhabitants of the French village that the bombs remained undetonated. Killem crawled out of the wreck, looked ruefully at the church spire, and muttered, "I've always

26

felt that I should have gone oftener to church in my youth. Now look at the damned result of my negligence."

It was Killem who tested out a new aeroplane one day while a south wind equal to the air speed of his machine was blowing. While flying north he travelled over the ground twice as fast as he travelled through the air, but when he turned around over the city of Toul he remained stationary. He was travelling through the air as fast as before, but now he was headed south, and as the wind passed over the ground toward the north as rapidly as Killem travelled through the air toward the south, the inhabitants of Toul were amazed to see a heavier-than-air machine remaining stationary above their heads. This situation greatly alarmed a dear old lady of Toul, who eventually arrived at our aerodrome in a donkey cart with the astounding information that one of our planes "had run out" of petrol and was stalled directly above her house.

CHAPTER 3

The Bedouins at Ochey Aerodrome

If you had visited the Bedouin Squadron at about eleven o'clock in the morning you would have received quite a shock when entering the officers' mess. In the first place, you would have found the mess deserted except for several dogs of unknown species and innumerable cats,—some proudly nourishing recent offspring, others in various stages of anticipation of a similar pleasure. Secondly, you would have been surprised at the comfortable, if not artistic, interior of our exteriorly unattractive hut. In the centre of the "ward-room" or sitting-room was an open fireplace of ingenious design. On a stone and earth base, covered with sheet iron, rested a large cast-iron box with many peculiarly shaped apertures resembling as far as possible the incomprehensible design of a lady's lace *mouchoir*. The fire-box was supported by four cast-iron "whirly-gigs," the artistic effort of a mechanic detailed to construct legs for the support of the aforesaid fire-box.

Above this box a large hollow pyramid, the apex of which connected with a pipe, which in turn after divers wanderings led through a hole in the roof, offered an exit for the smoke. Needless to say, this offer was frequently ignored. Around this fireplace was a foot-railing constructed from the main spar of a crashed Handley-Page. The rest of the furniture fortunately was not homemade. Large easy-chairs and lounges, the gift of a friendly merchant of Nancy, often made progress from one end of the room to the other,—a feat requiring considerable skill in navigation. A piano was wedged into one corner of the room; "Sin-fin," a mad Irishman, appeared with this piano one day together with an exhilarated French officer driving a lorry. No one ever found out how the piano had been secured, but since a sweet little "demoiselle" now rides "Sin-fin's" Irish hunters, we may believe, if we wish, that a rickety piano formed the basis of an international romance.

ENTRANCE TO OFFICERS' MESS

The walls of the room were draped with rich damask; as the officers' steward who produced this incongruous luxury was an ex-convict, no inquiries were made concerning it.

In the same hut with the ward-room and adjoining it was the mess or dining-room and beyond this was the "galley" or kitchen. While the Bedouins were inflicted with a cook who had been in pre-war days an expert electrician, the kitchen would not have been your most attractive route to the officers' sleeping-quarters.

Presuming that you left the mess through its more congenial exit, the ward-room, the next hut you would have come to was the officers' quarters. There at eleven o'clock in the morning you would have heard a full symphony rendered by twenty lusty sleepers. "Is this war?" you might have asked yourself if you did not have in mind that you were visiting a night-bombing squadron. The officers in this hut had returned but five or six hours previously from an all-night raid over Germany.

Beyond this hut are the men's quarters which are deserted at this hour. Across the road is the workshop or repair factory which, under the eye of "Bill," the engine officer, runs "full blast" from six in the morning to nine or ten at night. Next to this miniature factory is the armorers' hut where all the machine guns are overhauled daily, ammunition tested as regards rims, sunken caps, etc., and every possible precaution taken to render the guns thoroughly efficient.

Nearby are the huge, camouflaged hangars, or buildings containing the aeroplanes. Here the mechanics are "tuning up" the engines; the riggers are trueing up the aeroplanes, tightening a flying wire here, loosening a landing wire there, testing controls; in fact, doing all that scientific knowledge and care can do to reduce the chance of accident from mechanical imperfection. And upon these patriotic, scientific mechanics, working for their country and their ideals and recompensed from a pecuniary point of view with a shilling or two a day, rested to a large extent, the lives of the aviators and the success of their various adventures.

Back of the hangars and near the officers' quarters is the squadron office. Here are several clerks constantly engaged in recording all the details relating to the men's pay, their military records, their issues of clothes, blankets, etc.,—in fact, recording and filing everything dealing with the squadron's activities.

Next to the squadron office is the large map-room. If a squadron on active service can be compared to the human body, the map-room is the brain of the squadron, for here is kept all the information essential to the aviators. On one wall is a huge map of the whole war zone from the coast to the Swiss border. On this the front-line trenches are accurately marked, with their changes made from day to day. On the wall next to this map and at right angles to it, is a large-scale map of the entire region over which the squadron operates. On this map are numerous conventional markings which would have no meaning to the casual observer.

In maps of the enemy territory are hundreds of red drawing-pins. These mark the positions of enemy anti-aircraft batteries. As soon as information is received of the movement of one of these batteries, the pin which represents that particular battery is moved to the new position. Small yellow squares or oblongs with minute black marks represent the enemy aerodromes and hangars. These conventional signs correspond accurately to the aerial photographs of these aerodromes.

Small blue crosses represent the position of enemy balloon barrages and their height. The position of these barrages must be known accurately, for to run into them is fatal and at night they are very apt to trap the unwary. Roughly, they are a series of balloons supporting a huge wire net or cable streamers. The balloons, anchored to the ground and carrying the nets with them, are sent up to a considerable altitude about large cities and important industrial centres. They are to the night aviators what the spider's web is to the fly.

Another conventional sign of this map which is always puzzling to the uninitiated is a series of small pins with streamers attached. These streamers are marked with green dots. One streamer will have one green dot, another two green dots, another three, etc., while others will have different spaces between the dots. These pins mark the position of what is called the "Hun green-ball batteries," and these green balls, fired up to a height of about six thousand feet, direct the Hun aviators to their respective aerodromes when returning from a night raid.

A better system than this for directing aviators at night has never been devised, for low clouds or mist cannot obliterate the signal and they are visible to the aviator for over fifty miles. In fact, this type of signal was so very excellent that our knowledge of the exact positions of the various batteries was of great assistance to us in our raids over Germany.

On our side of the lines this map was marked with conventional signs similar to those which marked the position of enemy anti-air-

craft batteries, aerodromes, and balloon barrages; but on our side of the lines there were large areas marked in red to indicate what was called "prohibited areas"; *i.e.,* areas over which no aeroplane, Allied or enemy, could fly without being subjected to the fire of our anti-aircraft batteries.

There were also white drawing-pins, each bearing a letter, placed at irregular intervals. These located accurately the position of small lighthouses which are usually about fifteen miles apart and from three to ten miles back of the front-line trenches; the letter marked on each drawing-pin designates the letter flashed in Morse code by that particular lighthouse. This system of signals, used by the British to direct their night aviators to their aerodromes when returning from a raid, had but two great faults. In the first place, the signal was obliterated by low clouds and mist. In the second place, the flash of the light only carried a few miles even under the best conditions. On the other hand, the letters which the lighthouses flashed could be readily changed and consequently were of very little assistance to Hun aviators.

On the third wall of the map-room are aerial photographs of enemy aerodromes, railway stations, sidings, etc., and large-scale plans of German towns and factories.

On the table in the centre of the room are the various instruments by the aid of which the aviators are enabled to figure out their magnetic courses. Every afternoon the map-room is crowded with aviators. Here all the plans for the raid are made, the courses figured and marked on individual charts, the photographs or plans of targets studied and the best methods of approaching the target discussed. In the evening the wind soundings made by the meteorological expert are reported and again the map-room is crowded with aviators figuring out "drift" and "ground speed" and making out charts which will facilitate their navigation when in the air.

CHAPTER 4

A Night Raid

Every precaution having been taken, the engines run, the controls tested, the compasses swung, the courses made out, the charts prepared, and the drift figured, the Bedouins sat down to dinner free from care or worry. The dinner hour was always set, winter or summer, at least two hours before the night's raid was to start.

A guest of the Bedouin mess on the night of an important raid would have been surprised if told that the jolly, laughing officers, who apparently had no thought in the world other than the enjoyment of various wines and viands, were soon to set out on a pioneer raid against a far-distant German industrial centre. For the Bedouins made the best of the present; they all knew what a long-distance raid over Germany usually meant; many of their jolly comrades would not be seen again. So they made merry at dinner and drank each other's health. The wine, however, was light, and even the most reckless Bedouin drank it in tiny sips, for the work to be done was important. The personal dangers of the raid the reckless Bedouins might ignore, but they knew that these raids fitted into the general tactical plan of operations; consequently, every Bedouin was imbued with a spirit of determination in spite of an apparent frivolity.

On entering the ward-room a few moments before dinner, the guest of the Bedouin mess would have been greeted joyfully by the officers who were singing lustily in perfect tune with a piano which was very much out of tune. A few moments later he would see these rollicking fellows stand silently at attention on the entry of the commanding officer until "Good-evening, gentlemen," from the C.O. granted them permission to "carry on."

Before the chief steward announced dinner, "*apéritifs*" were passed around; then the C.O. led the way from the ward-room into the adjoining mess, where the officers stood at attention on each side of the long table until the C.O. said, "Gentlemen, be seated." If anyone came in late to dinner, he apologized to the C.O. before taking his place at the table; and no matter how oily and dirty he may have been a few moments earlier, he entered the mess clean, freshly shaven, and in neat uniform. This mess etiquette, as it was called, did not interfere in any way with the good-fellowship existing between the C.O. and his junior officers; but it prevented men who had been away from home and the society of ladies for many years from growing lax in manners and careless of personal appearance.

After dinner, decanters of port were passed around and the king's health was drunk: "Gentlemen, The King."

This toast means nothing to us Americans unless we have drunk it among British officers at the front. Under such conditions, "Gentlemen, The King," is a call to patriotism, a spur to endeavour, and an ideal of courage which must be lived up to. We Americans are so apt to think of a king as a despot or tyrant that it takes us a long time to understand the love which the Englishman has for his king. The King of England is as much of a symbol to Englishmen as the Stars and Stripes are a symbol to us. The king, as an individual, has no power, except the power of influence. This power is great when the influence exerted is in the right direction, but the king has no dictatorial power similar to that which may be granted to our Presidents. The king is merely a symbol which stands in the minds of Englishmen for patriotism, justice, democracy, and humanity. So when the Bedouins raised their glasses to the toast, "Gentlemen, The King," they paid a tribute to all that Great Britain and her Allies were fighting for—democracy, justice, and freedom of the individual from oppression.

After this final toast, every aviator went to his quarters and clambered into his bulky but warm flying clothes. There was no hurry or bustle, but each aviator, thoroughly equipped for the raid with maps, charts, and instruments, arrived at the map-room on a definite moment. Here he received a few final instructions from the commanding officer; then, smoking a last cigarette, he made his way through the dusk to his own aeroplane.

While the aviators drank to "Gentlemen, The King," the mechanics were warming up the twin motors of each aeroplane, the bomb-racks were being filled with fourteen one-hundred-and-twelve-pound bombs, the guns were being mounted, and by the time the aviators arrived on the aerodrome the huge Handley-Page bombing planes were in readiness for a nine hours' flight over Germany.

After climbing up a ladder to their respective positions, the aviators made a final survey of the machine on the reliability of which depended the success of their adventure. The engines were again run up to see that they gave the proper revolutions, the gauges inspected, the controls tested, and the return spring of each gun weighed. When thoroughly satisfied, each aviator took his place and his pilot signalled for the "chocks" to be withdrawn from in front of the wheels.

While the aviators carried on this final inspection of their machines, the aerodrome officer, stationed on a high platform situated in one corner of the field, awaited the signal to light the "landing T"; *i.e.*, a huge "T" of electric lights headed into the wind, which shows to the aviators the taking-off and landing path. Each machine is given its respective letter for the day, which is flashed in Morse code on the navigation lights by the aviator when ready to leave the ground; he then awaits an answer from the directing stand. Simultaneously with the lighting up of the huge "landing T," the letter flashed from the first machine ready is repeated by the signal officer. The answer received, the machine taxies across the aerodrome to the starting-point, turns, hurtles down the flare-path and leaves the ground at the head of the "T." Under this simple method of direction I have seen twenty aeroplanes leave an aerodrome on a pitch-black night in twelve minutes without a single mishap.

On leaving the ground the aeroplanes fly dead into the wind for a couple of miles, circle back to the left around the aerodrome, and head into the wind again until the height at which the flight is to be carried out is reached. The first aeroplane to reach this height passes directly over the aerodrome and then steers a course to the first lighthouse. A comparison of this course with the previously figured course, and a comparison of the previously calculated ground speed with the time taken to travel from the aerodrome to the lighthouse enables the aviators, by the use of instruments and a few simple calculations, to gauge their drift. This process is continued on another course to the next lighthouse and the previously tested direction and velocity of wind are accurately checked in this way and future courses altered accordingly.

These calculations are all important to the long-distance night bomber, for although roads show up in the moonlight like white threads, they are too numerous and interwoven to be followed for great distances, and although rivers and lakes look like silver ribbons and blotches, the moon may be obscured at any moment or the ground itself may be obliterated by low clouds or mist. Accuracy in aerial navigation, therefore, is of the utmost importance in long-distance night flying.

The night aviator, however, has many things to think of besides a constant checking and readjustment of his course according to variations in direction and velocity of wind. On his own side of the lines he is constantly challenged by searchlights which must be answered immediately if the aviator wishes to avoid the risk of being shot down by his own anti-aircraft guns or of being attacked by his own night-patrol machines. The method of answering these challenges is extremely simple. All that is required of the aviator is to shoot at the searchlight with a large pistol loaded with an enormous cartridge. The aviator, intent on his calculations and annoyed by any interruption, often wishes that this pistol was a deadly weapon, but it is not.

It merely fires a certain coloured light which floats slowly down changing in its descent to certain other colours, which prove to the officer in charge of the challenging searchlight that an Allied aeroplane is above him. The colours which are shown on one night, however, will not do on another, for these "colours of the day," as they are inappropriately called, are changed every night and the utmost secrecy is maintained in regard to them. Even the aviators do not know the "colour of the day" until ten minutes before the start of a raid, neither do the officers in charge of the anti-aircraft batteries. The reason for this secrecy became apparent to the Bedouins one night when a Hun flew over our aerodrome shooting down our "colour of the day," blinking his navigation lights, and finally firing down a red light which was our prearranged forced-landing signal. The aerodrome officer, believing that one of the Bedouin machines was returning from that night's raid with engine trouble, lit up the "landing T" and brought upon himself a shower of bombs which carried him into the Unknown.

After crossing the lines, the aviators are intent on steering an accurate compass course, checking their position from time to time by various landmarks such as canals, rivers, cross-roads, and woods, and figuring changes in wind. The bursting shells of the enemy anti-aircraft batteries must be disregarded, for a slight *détour* around a particularly heavy barrage might mean an error of several degrees in their course which, unless corrected, would bring them twenty to thirty miles away from their objective after a flight of one hundred and seventy miles or more, and an accurate correction of a compass course after a wide *détour* is always difficult and sometimes impossible. Therefore, it is of the utmost importance for long-distance night bombers to hold their course regardless of the enemy's efforts at destruction.

The hatred in the hearts of the Huns, expressed by the constant "*whonk*" of bursting anti-aircraft shells, contrasts disagreeably with the loveliness of the moonlit panorama. All man's disfigurements of the earth are obliterated by distance and nothing but a scene of inspiring beauty is in view from the aviators' lofty outlook at a height of several thousand feet.

The flashings of the guns, the "flaming onions,"—*i.e.*, strings of phosphorus balls shot up to light the sky and to ignite any inflammable substance with which they come in contact,—and the black puffs of smoke from the bursting shells add a weird and startling brilliancy to the surroundings. No matter how many times a man may fly at night the immensity of the heavens above him, crowded with unknown worlds, cannot fail to impress him with his own insignificance in the general scheme of the universe, and Death itself appears of small importance compared to the way in which he faces it.

The aviators, however, have little time for reflection, for on a long flight they must keep a constant outlook for such landmarks as will enable them from time to time to mark their exact position on the chart and by comparison with their compass course and "ground speed" vary their course according to changes in direction and velocity of wind. An instrument called the "pitot tube" indicates the speed at which the aeroplane passes through the air, but the speed at which the plane travels in relation to the ground depends on the direction and velocity of the wind. They must also watch the flashes from anti-aircraft batteries and pin-point them on their maps if possible; aerodromes which are lit up, train movements, the lighting of towns, the blaze of steel factories; in fact, everything of military importance must be recorded and reported upon, if accurately located.

The night aviator, however, must be extremely careful in his observations, for it is very easy to get lost and it is extremely difficult to keep an accurate check, on the charts, of your exact position over the ground, even after long practice; especially is this true when the flight covers three to four hundred miles in distance and lasts from eight to nine hours.

After several hours of intense concentration, the aviators approach their target, and although they have charted the course constantly they now spend some time in flying back and forth while they check off on a large-scale map the landmarks about the target and satisfy themselves that their long flight will not be valueless if the bombs are dropped with accuracy. In the meantime, the sound of the motors, together with the telegraphed intelligence from other Hun towns, tells the enemy that Allied night bombers are in the vicinity. The Huns in charge of the anti-aircraft defences stationed about the target direct huge beams of numerous searchlights toward the sky and an intense barrage is put up above and around the target by the Hun batteries. The air is filled with shrapnel from bursting shells at the altitude at which the machine is flying, for the Huns have accurate instruments which gauge the altitude of an aeroplane from the sound vibrations of its engines.

The aviators, however, are still intent on picking out their target (probably a factory which manufactures war material) and have not yet entered the barrage. The Huns, I imagine, often wondered why British bombers flew about a town for such a long time before bombing; the inhabitants always had more than enough time to enter the dug-outs before the bombs dropped. The British bombers, however, were not making war on women and children; they were intent on destroying a poisonous gas factory or other targets of military importance; so they flew about the town until the target was accurately located; then and not till then, they throttled down their engines and glided swiftly down between the searchlight beams and below the barrage of bursting shells, for once the engines are throttled down the enemy's sound instruments are valueless and the anti-aircraft barrage ranged at the previous altitude of the aeroplane fills the air with shrapnel far above the rapidly descending plane.

A quick adjustment of bomb-sights to compensate for the altitude, speed, and drift of the plane and the front fore-sight soon is in line with the target, and after a pause the back fore-sight coming in line with the back-sight gives, with the previously adjusted stop-watch, the exact moment for releasing the first bombs. The plane passes over the target and turns on a steep "bank," while the aviators watch for the burst of the bombs. The bomb-sight is readjusted to the reduced altitude, another sight taken, the remainder of the bombs released, and then, nose down, engine "full out," the huge plane rushes through the lowered barrage for more congenial surroundings.

Great care must be taken when bombing a factory, for usually very close to it the Hun has located an unprotected prison camp filled with

Allied prisoners, and we have official information that prisoners have so infuriated the Hun guards by singing "God save the King" or the "*Marseillaise*" during a bombardment of the near-by factory that they have been bayoneted to punish them for their "insolence." As soon as the aviators are away from the barrage, they steer a straight course for home, and again an intent outlook is kept for landmarks which will enable them to mark their position on the charts and figure their ground speed and drift. If their course is correct, they will see after a few hours a lighthouse several miles away dimly flashing a letter in Morse code. They head straight for this, and when over it they steer a course which will bring them to the lighthouse situated near their aerodrome.

As they approach the aerodrome they fire down the "colour of the day" and if the aerodrome is not under bombardment by the Huns the flare-path is lighted and the pilot spirals slowly down while the allotted letter of the plane is being flashed in Morse code on its navigation lights; as soon as this signal is answered from the ground, the pilot glides swiftly down to the flare-path. When fifteen to ten feet from the ground the Holt's flares attached to the wing tips of the planes are lit by electrical contact and the landing is made in a momentary but brilliant blaze of light.

It is interesting to sit in the officers' mess of a night-bombing squadron and watch the returning aviators enter. They are cold and stiff and all are very tired, for no man can fly without fatigue from dusk to dawn under conditions which demand intense concentration and entail a considerable amount of nervous strain, but now is shown the difference in temperament; some return with bloodshot eyes and haggard faces which indicate a condition of intense fatigue; others come in gaily as though home from a late dance; still others thoughtfully quiet. All of them, however, show signs of nervous strain and mental tension and they must relax their taut nerves before going to bed, especially if the raid was but another similar to those that had been carried out on several previous nights.

So, while relaxing they eat bully beef sandwiches and drink hot chocolate or beer or, if the night has been particularly cold, a glass of hot rum. Deafened by the roar of the engines and the sudden change in atmospheric pressure they either whisper or yell if they speak at all, during the first few minutes after entering the mess. But the raid is over, so very little is said about it; every now and then someone looks at his watch and sees that nine hours have elapsed since the raid started; he says nothing but he and all realize that the machine which has not returned has used up its supply of petrol and that the fate of a dear friend will remain unknown perhaps for weeks, perhaps for all time.

CHAPTER 5

Some Epics of Night Bombing

1

In the summer of 1917 the Germans were rushing troops up to the Ypres front, where the activities of the British threatened them at this point in their line. This movement of troops was made at night, as usual, *because* if made in daylight they would have been plainly visible to our reconnaissance and artillery observation squadrons. These troops were detrained at Menin and were transported by motor lorry along the Menin-Gelevelt road. On a certain evening the first night-bombing squadron of the Royal Flying Corps, then situated west of Nieppe Forest, was ordered to delay in every possible way this movement of enemy troops. The result must have been satisfactory, for the general in command of the British Army on that front sent us, a few days later, the glad tidings that no German reinforcements arrived at the critical moment and all the British objectives had been captured and held. Whether or not the only night-bombing squadron engaged in that action was responsible for the tie-up of the Hun transportation system is problematical, but all the members of the squadron remember that night and hope that their efforts were of value.

The only thing out of the ordinary that evening in the squadron's routine was the mounting of double guns in the aeroplanes and an earlier dinner hour; the dinner, possibly, was gayer than usual. The machines left the ground in daylight, gained their height over Nieppe Forest and crossed the lines at dusk, swooped down over Menin Station and dropped their bombs at an altitude of one thousand to five hundred feet. Then, nose down, engine "full out," they raced away from Menin and followed, in the brilliant moonlight, the road to Gelevelt, flying within one hundred feet of the ground.

A heavy fire at close range at the transports on the road and at the shadows of the trees cast by the moon, as the case might be, soon exhausted the drums of ammunition. Each aviator did his level best to get results, all the time trying to avoid landing on the tree-tops; some of them did so land; they were shot down by the Huns. As soon as their ammunition was gone they headed for home and, crossing the lines at a low altitude, were shot at by anti-aircraft batteries and machine guns from the ground and "bumped" here and there by the air displacement of passing shells from the steadily flashing guns of both their own and the enemy's artillery.

When they arrived at their aerodrome there was a breathing-spell for the aviators while the bomb-racks were being refilled with bombs, the empty ammunition drums replaced with full ones, and the engines replenished with petrol, oil, and water. The planes then roared into the air again, climbed for a short time, and then headed for Menin, where railway communications were again bombed and the Menin-Gelevelt road was again raked with machine-gun fire.

After a brief respite on the return from this second raid, the machines again took off and raided the Huns for the third time that night. All that were left of this weary group of aviators returned from this third raid in broad daylight, with nerves strained to the verge of a breakdown; some were in tears, some striving to be gay, and some were very quiet, but all happy in knowing that they had "done their damndest."

When afterward they learned that the "push" had been successful and that the Hun reserves had failed to appear, their grief for the "missing" was softened by the thought that *their* sacrifice had not been in vain; it had brought about the full accomplishment of the purpose of the raids—*C'est la Guerre*—

2

Probably the first time that a Rhine town was bombed on a densely cloudy night was in the spring of 1918 and it was bombed by a small Scotchman called "Jock."

The wind that night was from the northeast, a favourable wind from the aviators' point of view because it was against them on the outward voyage. Shortly after crossing the lines, however, dense clouds coming up with the wind obliterated the earth, and all the aviators except Jock turned back hoping to find their aerodrome before it was also blotted out by the low-lying clouds.

Jock, however, was "keen" on bombing Hun factories, and the objective that night was the Badische Works situated on the river Rhine; so Jock held to his compass course and flew for over four hours without once seeing the ground. When a sufficient time had elapsed to bring him over his target, if his previous reckoning, of course, of ground speed and drift was correct, and if the wind had not varied in velocity or strength, Jock "spiralled" down through the clouds and, finding the ground beneath him nothing but dense blackness, glided lower and lower until eventually a large town directly beneath him became visible and then the River Rhine, passing between Ludwigshafen on the west and Mannheim on the east, was lit up by the rays of the moon coming through a sudden rift in the clouds. Jock by now was only eight hundred feet above Mannheim; he opened up his throttle and circled around the city while his navigation officer on his large-scale chart compared the landmarks momentarily made visible by the rift in the clouds.

At last, thoroughly satisfied as to their position, fourteen one-hundred-and-twelve-pound bombs were dropped as near the factory as possible. If some of these bombs dropped in the town itself, it was not due to intention on the part of the aviators, who, blinded by searchlights, could not be sure of sending all the bombs with accuracy. With over one hundred and sixty miles to travel in a plane riddled with shrapnel from the bursting shells, the prominent thought in the minds of the aviators was, that their work being accomplished, their next move was to "beat it" in the direction where lay friendly country.

After the release of the bombs, Jock climbed up through the clouds and steered a direct course for home. Since the ground could not be studied because of the intervening clouds, the aviators devoted their entire attention to compass, time, and the stars. During this flight above the clouds the efficiency of the Hun's sound instruments was thoroughly demonstrated, for, although the clouds were too dense for any searchlight to penetrate and this effectually screened the machine from observation from below, again and again Jock's plane was surrounded by the black puffs of bursting anti-aircraft shells.

After flying for a sufficient number of hours to bring them above their aerodrome, if their calculations were correct, Jock and his companion discussed the advisability of coming down through the clouds; the unanimous decision, however, was to continue on until a lack of petrol would force them to land, for changes in wind might have created a considerable error in their calculations, unchecked as they were by observations of landmarks; so after flying for another hour they came down through the clouds and succeeded in making a safe landing near a small French village just before their supply of petrol was exhausted.

3

One evening in August, 1918, there was a strong southwest wind blowing across the eastern part of France and severe thunderstorms were reported to be approaching. Nevertheless, certain Bedouins were selected to raid the railway station and sidings at Frankfort; "intelligence" having reported important rail movements in that vicinity. The Bedouins were ordered to return if they found, after testing the air, the weather conditions unfavourable for a flight of such long distance. As an alternative target to Frankfort they were given the Burbach Hutte Works at Saarbrucken.

After gaining their height above the aerodrome, Jock and his navigation officer steered a direct course for "D" lighthouse, situated north of Barcarat and but a few miles from the front-line trenches. Having accurately figured their drift and ground speed on this course, Jock and his companion calculated that, by steering a straight course to Frankfort, spending five minutes over the target, and steering a straight course back to their aerodrome, they could make sufficient headway against the wind on the return voyage to bring them safely home with a ten minutes' supply of petrol left in their tanks; any error in course necessitating a deviation, or any increase in the velocity of the wind, might mean a prolonged *sojourn* in a German prison camp if not subjection to the well-known tortures of a German hospital.

After an accurate calculation of direction and velocity of wind, a course of thirty-nine degrees was steered from "D" lighthouse; the River Saar was crossed north of Saarburg; Bitsch and Pirmasens were passed to the north and Kaiserlautern to the south and then, the Vosges Mountains having been crossed, Jock and his companion looked down on the Rhine valley. The Rhine River was crossed north of Oppenheim, and from an elevation of six thousand feet, Mainz, at the juncture of the rivers Main and Rhine, showed clearly in the moonlight. Still holding their course, the aviators looked out to the left, followed up the River Main to Frankfort, here they throttled back the engines, glided swiftly down through the anti-aircraft barrage and searchlights and released their bombs as accurately as possible.

Then, after an almost vertical "bank" so sudden was the turn, Jock steered a straight course for the nearest point in the lines, which was considerably over one hundred miles away. Now the aviators had to face a strong head wind and steer straight into a rapidly approaching storm. The time taken to fly from Frankfort to the Rhine River, together with a change in drift, proved to the aviators that the wind had varied slightly in direction and had increased somewhat in velocity. They immediately decided not to lose time by climbing above the approaching storm, but to pass beneath it.

This they did, and those aviators never went through a nastier experience than this homeward journey. Blinded and stung as they were by the downpour of rain, while their aeroplane was hurled about by the wind to such an extent that it appeared to be completely out of control, the voyage seemed interminable. The clouds above belched flashes of lightning in apparent unison with the Hun anti-aircraft batteries below. Held in the beams of the enemy's searchlights and plainly visible against the dark clouds above, Jock's plane was an easy target for the Hun gunners.

But who can account for the fortunes of war? Jock brought his plane, riddled with shrapnel, into the moonlight beyond, showing up Kaiserlautern directly below, with its searchlights sweeping the sky while its anti-aircraft batteries filled the air with bursting shells; but in spite of this "hate" it was a pleasant sight to the aviators, for it showed them that their course was correct and that there was still time to gain the lines unless the wind increased. Again they passed below another dense bank of clouds, to experience again being blinded with the rain and shaken by the violence of the wind by which their plane was tossed about, all the while subjected to an attack by lightning from above and by anti-aircraft guns from below. It is a little trying to the nerves to fly for an hour without being able to see the earth beneath, and surrounded by the incessant flashings of lightning and the "*whonkings*" of bursting shells, but when homeward bound these little incidents are of minor import.

For the second time Jock brought the plane, tossing about like a cork on a mountainous sea, out into comparative light. As landmarks were recognized, the course was checked and changed, when a third storm was encountered. This last storm was furious, and it was impossible to hold the plane on a compass course; fortunately, however, the storm lasted but a short time, and when Jock brought his plane out into the breaking dawn, the Marne-Rhine Canal was visible to the south. A few moments later the lines were crossed and a direct course

AFTER THE LANDING

was steered to the nearest aerodrome. Just then the engines spluttered, then stopped, the petrol was exhausted, and Jock was forced to land in a field near Lunéville after a sustained flight of eight hours and fifty minutes.

CHAPTER 6

The Guiding Hand

Mysterious Dick, or "Mystery" as he was usually called, was a slender, anaemic-looking boy with deep brown eyes. He was nicknamed "Mystery" for several reasons. In the first place, he gave everyone on first acquaintance an uncomfortable feeling; no one could explain this, but everyone admitted that he was a "bit queer." When he looked at you his eyes never appeared to be focused on you, but to be looking at something back of you; I have seen a man to whom Dick was talking suddenly turn and look over his shoulder. Another very noticeable trait of Dick's was to answer an unasked question, or to interrupt a man at the beginning of an argument with a refutation or agreement, as the case might be.

I remember coming into the mess one morning about five o'clock after an all-night raid; our machine was the third back. It was a bitter cold winter's night and "upstairs" it was absolutely numbing. In the mess there were Mac and Dick and one or two others, thawing their congealed blood and numbed brains with hot rum. It had been a nasty trip that night, dense, low clouds and a head wind on the return voyage; there were many machines still unaccounted for, although the supply of petrol would "keep them up" but another fifteen minutes. So in the mess we sipped our hot rum and sat and thought, or just sat.

"I think they were south of Dieuze"; it was Dick who broke the silence.

Mac jumped and looked hard at "Mysterious Dick," and as we all looked at him inquiringly a faint flush rose to his face, he gulped down his rum and left the mess.

"It's queer," said Mac, "how often he does that."

"Does what?" I asked.

"Answer your unasked question," replied Mac. "The green balls must have been south of Dieuze just as 'Mystery' said, for after leaving Mannheim I followed up the Rhine to Hagenau Wald, turned west and crossed the Vosges over Zabern; here we went above low clouds and I didn't see the ground again for over an hour. I steered my course all right, but was fearing a change of wind when just ahead of me I saw the Hun signal of two green balls come up through the clouds; as the last 'intelligence' placed these two balls at Morchange, I changed my course from 270° to 245°. It was only luck that about half an hour later a rift in the clouds showed me 'F' lighthouse, and as that is about thirty miles south of 'B' lighthouse, my original course over Zabern of 270° must have been about right to strike 'B' lighthouse. So the green-ball signal, as 'Mystery' said, must have been moved from Morchange to south of Dieuze, and that is just what I was puzzling out when Dick answered the puzzle for me. He's queer, all right." And Mac called for another rum.

And "queer" is the best description of Dick that any of the Bedouins could have given you, if you had asked them, until one night he was finally coaxed after many "treats" to tell about his earlier war experiences. Dick said quietly:

In 1912 I was a subaltern in the Indian Army, a row over a woman resulted in my court martial and disgrace.

When the war broke out I joined as a dispatch rider; I was wounded and was in the hospital for over five months. When I came out I succeeded in getting into the Royal Flying Corps and eventually was granted a commission. But as a pilot I was a complete failure; I 'wrote off' several machines and in my last crash I nearly 'wrote off' myself. I was unconscious for over a month and it was over eight months before I left the hospital.

I finally got back to France as a recording officer to a Handley-Page squadron; here I ran into an old pal of mine, and one night, when his navigation officer was sick, my pal took me on a raid without saying a word to anyone. It was the first time I had ever been in a Handley-Page aeroplane and it was the first time I had ever flown at night, but my pal was the best pilot in the squadron and the way to the Gontrode aerodrome was an open book to him, for he had been there many times before; he took me as a passenger for the experience.

I remember as we 'taxied' over the aerodrome that the roar of the engine on each side of me, the flashing of lights, the other machines as they passed us or waited with slowly 'ticking-over props' for us to pass, the different-coloured lights which were being fired down from machines already in the air and the lights fired up from the ground, all combined and whirled through my excited brain like a meaningless nightmare. Then there was a deafening roar and we shot down a path of light, bumped hard, bumped less hard, bumped again, and the huge plane with its great load of bombs was in the air. Lights on the ground and the lights of machines in the air became mixed until I could not tell one from the other.

As we rose higher and higher, ground lights far off in the distance came hurtling toward us like the navigation lights of a fast approaching machine; I would clutch Jack, yell, and point out the lights in order to avoid a collision as it seemed to me; Jack would grin, pull me down on the seat beside him, and tell me the lights were on the ground and at least ten miles away. Gradually I got control of myself and tried to find the aerodrome we had just left; it was nowhere to be seen. There was a network of white threads on a black background, an occasional winding silver ribbon with here and there a silver blotch and queer-shaped blacker blacknesses on the general blackness; these were roads, rivers, lakes, and woods as they looked from the air at night.

How long we had been in the air I don't know. Time seemed nothing, or an eternity. We were suspended in a sphere. Lights or stars rushed at us or receded or whirled about. Time and distance became mere words without meaning and I had fallen into a state resembling hypnotic sleep when suddenly roused by Jack. 'There are the lines,' he shouted, and as far as the eye could see, to left and right, out of the darkness beneath us were the constant flashes of the never silent guns of the Flanders front. Every now and then we got a sudden 'bump' as a shell passed near us. I had fallen into an almost semiconscious state when 'tut-tut-tut-tut-tut' jumped me off my seat; I realised that I was surrounded by a dazzling whiteness; the machine itself was brilliant. Amidst the 'tut-tut-tut' of our own machine guns shooting down at the searchlights there was a constant dull 'whonk,' 'whonk,' 'whonk,' and the whole machine seemed to be enveloped in puffs of black smoke as the anti-aircraft batteries found the range.

Suddenly the nose of the machine went down and my breath

left me in the crazy rush, my hands grasped at anything, and somehow, momentarily blinded with fright as I was, my right hand involuntarily clutching Jack conveyed the truth to my brain. Jack was dead. He had fallen forward on the wheel and the giant plane was rushing, roaring down to destruction. With a spasmodic effort I pulled his body from the seat onto the floor at my feet and pulled back the wheel. With a sickening change and a shrill singing of wires we were climbing. How the fuselage and tail plane stood the strain of it, God knows. I was in Jack's seat now pushing the wheel from me, pulling it toward me, turning it to the right, then to the left, pushing the rudder bar with my right foot, then with my left. Panic was in control. We must have dropped three thousand feet before a sudden calmness came over me and I found this aerial monster as gentle to manage as a perfectly bitted horse.

But there was Jack, huddled on the floor at my feet with part of his head gone. I remember leaning down and trying to pull him out of his cramped position, and then came an eternity of stargazing. I wondered why the stars didn't run into each other and crash. I leaned across the fuselage and turned a pet-cock; a little spray of petrol came out with the escaping air; the hands of two dials on the left side of the cock-pit began turning slowly anti-clockwise; I forgot them and looked at the stars. Later I pressed a button on the dashboard and looked out at my starboard engine; a small dial was lit up. I looked at the port engine, a similar dial was lit up. I took my right hand from the wheel and pulled the throttle slightly back; again I star-gazed as if in a dream and without any volition I closed the pet-cock which I had previously opened.

This was my first time in a Handley-Page, and I knew nothing of pressures or temperatures. How long I flew I don't know; what direction I should have flown I did not know at that time. Occasionally I glanced at the compass and as well as I can remember the needle pointed west generally, but I gave it no thought. Finally, I pulled back the throttle and began to glide. I leaned over the next seat and pulled two levers. Remember that at this time I had never heard of shutters for the radiators. Down I came into heavier and heavier atmosphere. I was calm and happy. I never even gave the ground a thought, never even glanced at it. I remember taking from a rack on my left a stubby revolver with a huge bore, pointing it over the side and pulling the trigger, and I watched a green light go slowly down and searchlights that were blinking up at me went out.

A few seconds later a knob on the dashboard seemed to rivet my attention; it was a small knob exactly like an electric-light switch. I began to play with this. To do this I had to lean forward and stretch out my left arm; this action brought my face around to the right, and as I played with the knob I saw a light blinking on my right wing tip. I remember laughing at this.

The plane took a sudden dip and I sat up. Just off to my right and very little below me were lights on the ground in the shape of a 'T,' and other lights were flashing at me. I turned toward the 'T' and stuck down the nose of the machine; I pulled the throttle farther back, and just as I seemed to be running into dense blackness I leaned forward and pressed a button; a brilliant light sprang up under the machine; there was the ground not two feet away, apparently. I yanked back the wheel and a moment later there was a great bump, another and another, and we came to rest on our own aerodrome.

The doctor told me that he had never seen such a collapse. I had been unconscious for hours after being lifted from the machine together with my dead pal. I was awarded this decoration, gentlemen, for bringing that machine home safely. Since that time I have been awarded these other decorations for feats you have all heard of. But I want to tell you," and "Mystery Dick" stood up with flushed face and blazing eyes, "that I have never flown an aeroplane in France. Jack, my old pal, dare-devil Jack, whose head was blown off beside me during my first trip across the lines, flies my machine. Jack, dear old Jack, has won these medals I wear.

And Dick, no longer "Mystery Dick," left the mess. I say no longer "Mystery Dick" because from that day on there was nothing mysterious about Dick to the "Bedouins."

Explain it as you may, call it God, the spirit of a dead friend, or a thought vibration to which their mind is attuned, explain it as you choose, or try to explain it not at all, every member of the "Bedouin" Squadron has felt the "Guiding Hand" and every "Bedouin" knew, as every man who makes constant companions of danger and death must eventually know, that the dead still "carry on."

Three Accounts from *New England Aviators 1914-1918*

LIEUT. SAMUEL P. MANDELL

A Bit of Unintentional "Acrobatics"
By Lieut. Samuel P. Mandell

(Account of how his observer, Lieut. Fiske, was thrown from his plane when two thousand feet in the air.)

I had the thrill of my life yesterday. We were flying formation in these great big busses and the machine I had had, two camera guns on it, one for the pilot and one for the observer. Old F was standing up on the seat in back shooting away with his camera gun at a scout machine that was flying around us. At the same time, I dove to get a shot at him with my gun. I heard sort of a crash behind, and after I had straightened out looked around to see what it was. Lo and behold, a man in a leather coat holding onto the tail of my machine. I could hardly believe my eyes, but F had fallen out of his cockpit when his gun broke loose from its fastenings and I had nosed over. The first thought that came to me was: Will he have strength enough to hold on till I get down to the ground? I put the machine in the gentlest glide I could and started for home, as I could not land where I was up on the mountain-tops.

All this happened at about 700 metres. God help him if he had fallen. F all this time was lying with his body across the fuselage right next to the vertical stabilizer on the tail. As I watched him over my shoulder, he gradually wound his way up the fuselage. He got a-straddle of it and gradually slid up, caught hold of the tourelle, and dove head first into his seat. About ten years' weight came off my shoulders by this time. It was the funniest sight in the world to see the expression on that face as he scrambled up the fuselage and fell face first into the cockpit with only his heels sticking out. All that saved him was the little wooden spars that hold the covering of the fuselage breaking and making a sort of a hole in which his body stuck as it struck. As we were in formation, some of the other men saw it. They said that F left the fuselage bodily and flew through the air for a space of five feet till he struck the vertical stabiliser that knocked him back on to the fuselage. Of course, it is hard to believe, but it is Gospel truth. All the time it was happening we were going at the rate of 100 miles per hour at least.

F today is reposing in bed, having been excused from all formations. He will never come any nearer death at the front, and nothing can ever scare me any more than this did.

A Bit of Unintentional "Acrobatics"

How an Observer Was Thrown from His
Plane 2000 Feet in the Air
and Came Back

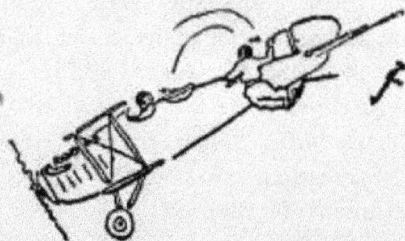

(Courtesy of the Lynn Item)

The Last Raid

By Lieutenant Gardiner Fiske

> Thirty of our bombing planes executed a successful raid on Moutons and Rawsourt this morning, dropping over two tons of bombs with good effect.—American *Communiqué* of Nov. 6.

To the Headquarters of the 1st Day Bombardment Group at Maulan, south of Bar-le-Duc on the evening of Nov. 4, came the daily telephonic order from General Headquarters. It was as usual a very simple order, giving nothing beyond the bare facts of the work the squadrons were to do the following day. This time the order said:

> Stand by to bomb Mouzon at 9.45 a.m.

On receiving this order, the flight leaders and deputy leaders went to their maps to locate the new objective and study photographs of the town to pick out the points of military value. In studying Mouzon it was not difficult to see what we were to do. The town lay on the east bank of the Meuse with a suburb on the west bank where the railroad station and warehouses were situated. We decided to try to cut the railroad and destroy the warehouses.

The next morning our orderlies called us early enough to see a low-lying mist over the camp. It was just dawn. We dressed amidst shouts from the barracks of "Come on, rain." This appeal to the rain god was heard every morning whatever the weather, as rain was sure preventive of bombing raids. Nevertheless, we felt that thrill which came only when we were on the alert to go over.

At 7.15 the flight leaders held their meeting in the office of the Group Commander, where the colonel outlined the plan of the formation to bemused. This morning, if the weather cleared up, we were to go over in three "V's," the 166th Squadron first, then the 20th, and lastly the 11th. We were to meet over our own field at 8000 feet, fall in behind one another in order, and climb to the final height of 13,000 to 14,000 feet during the final run to the lines. We were to bomb with the wind, which the weather report showed to be blowing toward Germany at a speed of about 30 miles an hour. This was rather a stiff wind, difficult but not impossible to operate in.

The sun appeared quickly, drying up the mist as if anxious to see us get on our way. We dressed carefully in our flying clothes, climbing into the De Havilands, and tested out our sights, machine guns, and Verys pistols. Soon the signal "all set" was given. A Verys pistol was fired showing one green ball, giving the signal to start the Libertys. With a roar the long line of engines started almost all at once as the mechanics swung the propellers and the process of warming up began. Then we—we were flight leaders that day in our squadron, the 20th—began taxiing to the starting-line; number 2 followed, then number 3, and so on until the whole flight were ready in formation on the ground—all the powerful engines throbbing and the propellers turning over. Suddenly the Operations Officer, noting the squadron ahead of us had left the field, fired a single red Verys light from the line. We opened our throttle and moved forward, taking off into the air. As we took off, numbers 2 and 3 started forward and in their turn leapt into the air, numbers 4 and 5 followed, then the next two and finally the 9th, until all the planes were in sight.

Our next difficulty was to gather the squadron into formation. After getting up to 1000 feet altitude, we throttled down until 2 and 3 caught up and climbed a little above and behind us. We three then continued climbing slowly until the rest gathered together and formed our "V" in a wide, loose formation.

The flight climbed together until we reached our desired altitude over the field. Taking one hour, this part of the trip is always very tiresome. One sits gazing at the altimeter, wondering if one will ever get up, the time passing so slowly. Down below the country gradually gets more and more spread out, until the forests blend into a patch of green and the rivers show only as nickled lines.

We returned over the field, looking meanwhile for the other two squadrons. Finally, down below us we saw the leaders, the 166th, starting for the lines. We fell in line behind them, passing over Bar-le-Duc and flying up the valley with the Argonne Forest on our left and Verdun on the right. As we neared the lines I signalled the planes into close formation so that by the time we crossed we were prepared to withstand an attack, the planes being stepped up and back with the

"V" much smaller. One plane here firing a red light fell out with motor trouble, not being able to keep up with our speed. We all had orders to return in this contingency.

The clouds were numerous and heavy, but we could see the leading squadron ahead as well as patches of ground in spots showing us our position. We were travelling at a terrific rate, the wind being apparently much stronger than the weather report showed. Stenay was plainly visible on our right. I thought of turning and dropping our bombs there, but as the leaders still went on I followed, thinking that they could see the objective from their position, though I could not see it from ours. As they reached the place where Mouzon was situated, they turned to the left over Raucourt, because, as we learned later, Mouzon was covered with clouds when they passed it. All this time the anti-aircraft shells were bursting around us, but our speed compared with the ground was so great that they were very inaccurate at our height of 14,000 feet. They showed, however, that we were discovered by the enemy and we could expect an attack by their planes.

As we reached Mouzon luck caused a sudden rift to appear in the clouds and the town was plainly visible. I steered the pilot, by the reins attached to his arms, for the town, swinging the formation to the right. Getting the edge of the town in the sight I gave the "all set" signal by firing off a Verys light with seven green balls. At this point always comes a tense moment. The town passed back along the bar of the sight, reached the cross-bar and passed it. I pulled back the lever and let go our bombs. Waiting a few seconds to be sure all the squadron had dropped theirs, I signalled to the pilot that all was well and to go home. Leaning over the side of the plane as far as possible, I tried to see the effects of the bursts, noticing one on a barracks and some flames near the railroad.

We turned now down the Meuse toward home against the wind, feeling that all was well. It had been a successful raid, and we were feeling happy about it.

Without warning a blue body with a white cross flashed up in front of us. Grasping a Verys light, always kept prepared, I gave the "Enemy Aircraft" signal—seven red balls—and stood up at the guns ready for the attack. The first Boche passed from under our wing and came up under our tail. I gave him one volley as he passed and continued as he hung on his propeller not twenty feet from us, just behind our horizontal stabilizer. In this volley I shot away our right flipper wires so that I had to be careful in the future in shooting on the other side, as if both sides were shot away we should be forced to land. This blue fellow went down some distance, but climbed up behind us again and reopened fire, his tracers flashing all around us, but never hitting any vital part.

The other planes in the formation were having their troubles too. From the leader's place I could see one Boche in flames above the rear of the formation and one Liberty going down below for protection. This plane was smoking, but not yet in flames. Then the fight stopped just as suddenly as it began. I counted the squadron, and slacking speed to gather the planes back into the "V," found there were seven left. We seemed to have got at least two Boches and had lost one of ours.

At this point two more German Squadrons appeared from the rear. The first thing I saw was one of our rear planes dive down suddenly into the middle of the "V" with two black-and-white-checked Fokkers after him. One of these fell out of control into a vrille; the other fell back and satisfied itself with long-distance firing; the Liberty went back to its old position. The tracers were flying by in the rear of the formation in all directions, but it was impossible to see exactly how many Boches were in the attack. One started crawling up on us from behind about twenty-five feet below. I fired bursts at him steadily, but he still came on. Having made a habit of always keeping one magazine in reserve on the gun fully loaded, I felt in the cockpit for a fresh one to replace the one just used up. There were none left. The reserve I had on the gun was now the last shot I had in the plane. As the German came nearer I fired in bursts of ten my last magazine. He turned back, luckily, as we were now helpless in case he persisted. I swung the useless tourelle back and forth pretending to point the guns at him as he hung back 400 yards behind. Finally, we seemed to crawl by Stenay and got over our lines at Dun-sur-Meuse. Here again I counted the flight. There were five left.

We arrived back at the field to await the hardest part of the whole raid. After making our report we watched the sky for the missing planes to come in. One hour passed; then two; finally, we heard a month later that one plane had gone down in flames and two others had been forced to land in German territory. This was our last raid, as the rain god answered our daily supplications from Nov. 6 to Nov. 11.

Samuel Pierce Mandell

Second First Lieutenant, A.S., U.S.A., Twentieth Aero Squadron, First Day Bombardment Group Killed in action, Nov. 5, 1918

Son of George S. and Emily (Proctor) Mandell; was born in Boston, Mass., March 20, 1897. A special slant was given his boyhood by an out-of-door environment. His days were spent in riding, hunting, breaking colts, and playing polo. He entered Harvard College from St. Mark's in 1915. His freshman vacation he devoted to the Harvard Flying Corps, going to Ithaca, N.Y., and the next spring enlisted at Newport News, March 3, 1917, though the U.S. had not then entered the war. Here he qualified as pilot July 25, and passed on to M.I.T., Cambridge, and Mineola, N.Y., where he received his commission, Nov. 5, 1917. Thence he proceeded overseas, Dec. 15.

Landing at Glasgow, he was sent to Winchester, and almost immediately to France: Issoudun, Jan. 25 to March 20; Tours, to May 21; Clermont-Ferrand, to July 11; Châteaudun, to Aug. 18; Orly, and finally on Aug. 30 was assigned to the 20th Aero Squadron and the front.

The very first flight over enemy lines which the 20th was asked to make was to take part in the St.-Mihiel drive. In driving rain and hail, weather such as none of them had ever before been permitted to venture out in, these untried men were sent to support the American attack. That they met the crisis splendidly is recorded in the citation which the group received, for having "shown a devotion to duty and initiative which has not been exceeded by any troops on the front."

Mandell participated in 17 raids, practically all that were made by the squadron, and for this he was cited. On the day before his last flight, he was certified for bringing down an enemy Fokker.

His last flight—and it was the last American air raid of the war— was on Nov. 5, Mouzun being the objective. A detailed account is given elsewhere. It was in the third fight that his "ship" shot up. An aileron was put out of commission and the engine was shot dead. The "ship," then some 12,000 feet up, sank in great spiral vrilles from which its occupants managed to right it about every 1000 feet. The last recovery was less than 100 feet from the ground. It fell within a few yards of the canal in Martincourt.

Lieut. R. W. Fulton, of N.Y., his observer, was practically unhurt; Mandell's leg was badly broken. The exact details of his other injuries are doubtful. The Germans marched Fulton away, and left the wounded pilot propped against his plane.

The rest of the story is gleaned from the inhabitants of the town. About 4 o'clock in the afternoon, a German captain of infantry came to the bank, took a rifle from one of the guards, and deliberately fired a number of shots into the helpless American.

It was the 17th before a detachment from the 5th Marines, in passing through the town, were notified of the dead young aviator. Reverently they buried him where he fell. Shortly afterward, the Meuse overflowed. It was thus that news came to Lieut. Petit, of the 58th Field Artillery, who had known Mandell at home as a fellow sportsman. Petit immediately arranged for a reinternment in a little country churchyard on the hill nearly opposite. Later, the body was again transferred to the little U.S. military cemetery between Beaumont and Letanne.

CITATIONS
(General Orders, No. 27)
November 17, 1918

First Lieutenants S. P. Mandell, John T. Willis, Jr., and Gardner H. Fiske and Second Lieutenant L. P. Koepfgen, 20th Aero Squadron, First Day Bombardment Group are hereby credited with the distinction, in combat, of an enemy Fokker, in the region southwest of Montmédy at 12,000 feet altitude, on November 4, 1918 at 15.25 o'clock.

By order of Col. Milling U. C. Sherman Lieut. Col. A.S., U.S.A., Chief of Staff

(General Orders, No. 29)
November 21, 1918

Extract

The Army Air Service Commander First Army cites the following officers and men for exceptional devotion to duty.

First Lieutenant S. P. Mandell, A.S., U.S.A., as Pilot of the 20th Aero Squadron, First Day Bombardment Group, participated in every raid made by the squadron in the Argonne-Meuse sector during October, 1918.

By order of Col. Milling U. C. Sherman Lieut. Col A.S., U.S.A., Chief of Staff .

A Happy Warrior

William Muir Russel

Contents

Who is the happy warrior? Who is he
That every man in arms should wish to be?
★★★★★★

He who, if he be called upon to face
Some awful moment to which Heaven has joined
Great issues, good or bad for humankind,
Is happy as a lover; and attired
With sudden brightness, like a man inspired.
Plays in the many games of life that one
Where what he most doth value must be won;
★★★★★★

This is the happy warrior; this is he
Whom every man in arms should wish to be.
—Wordsworth.

A Family Memorial

THE BIRTHPLACE

Foreword

The letters of William Muir Russel, Sergeant and First Lieutenant in the American Air Service, written home, tell the story of the training and experience of an American aviator in the great war. At his request, they were never published during his lifetime.

Now that he is gone, they are gathered in book form as a family memorial. The numerous pictures showing the winsome boy and man at different ages of his short life are included on account of the character of the book, which is issued privately only, and the fact that the letters are actual copies with the exception of a few elisions will excuse repetitions, and personal references and tributes which otherwise might be considered offenses to modesty. The names he mentions and things which may seem insignificant to others are given just as he wrote them.

Aside from the desire to keep his memory green and to gratify a just pride, the letters seem worthy of preservation as a contribution to the history of our country's preparation for war and participation in a new branch of the service. There seems to be inspiration in them, and here and there glimpses of premonition.

The history of the boy who gave his life so willingly is brief. He was born in the house which was his only home in Detroit, Michigan, on December 4, 1893, the youngest of five children, three sisters and a brother who died in his youth. He was named for his mother's father, William Muir. In his early infancy, he was nicknamed "Columbus" on account of the curious happening narrated in the letter contained in this book, written the day before he expected to sail for overseas service.

He was the first scholar and baby of the Detroit University School and a member of Gamma Delta Psi. In 1910, after his mother's death, he went to the Hill School, Pottstown, Pennsylvania, where he graduated in the class of 1913, and was editor-in-chief of the Dial, and a member of the students' governing committee. He went from there to Cornell University, and graduated in the class of 1917. The degree of Bachelor of Arts was conferred three months after he enlisted. He was a member of the Kappa Alpha Fraternity and some of the other leading organisations in college, in all of which, by reason of his popularity and traits of leadership, he held prominent office. He never took a high stand as a scholar, but was a well-posted, intelligent student, a good speaker, and an unusually fine, fluent writer.

From the time when he was a very little chap, a pad of paper and a long pencil were always part of his pocket equipment, and the leaves were filled with his beautiful handwriting and fine drawings. The habit continued with him in the use of his ever-ready fountain pen. There are seventy of his letters in this book, written on any old paper from wherever he happened to be during his fifteen months of service. Of course, he must have written many others.

He was a manly fellow, blessed with good health, a vigorous frame, and a receptive mind. He inherited the good looks and admirable traits of his charming, Christian mother. The family were Presbyterians and he was a member of that church.

He had a merry tongue in his head, and bubbled over with humour. The many stories of his childhood wit treasured in the family are delightful, and in any company and under all circumstances, he was an agreeable, desired companion. In his conversation, and in his letters written before he went to war, flashes of wit were frequent. He was voted the wittiest man in his class, and yet in all his letters contained in this book, there are few touches of humour. From a happy, carefree boy, he became, almost overnight, a serious man, intensely imbued with a sense of duty. There was also a physical change; from a vigorous stripling, he developed in five months into a robust man, adding nearly twenty pounds to his weight.

He had never engaged in any regular employment, and had hardly ever done any business work except in connection with his school, college and social activities, until he entered the service. He possessed rather exceptional mechanical skill and knowledge, especially of motors and electric and photographic apparatus, and seemed to grasp the science.

He was proficient in athletic sports and games, and was especially fond of angling and life in the woods. In his early boyhood he became his father's companion and fished many trout and salmon streams with him. His skill and engaging qualities made him welcome company with older men.

He was an expert swimmer, and just before he sailed overseas, remarked, "Take care of that copper cup which I won in the swimming contest at Gloucester. It is the only prize I ever took in my life." This fact may have been due to his extreme modesty, which was almost a drawback to him.

He had travelled somewhat extensively in the United States and Canada. His vacations were spent on the Fontinalis Stream in the Michigan woods, at Grosse Pointe on Lake St. Clair, and at the seashore. There was never a summer of his life until he went to war without some happy days along the Fontinalis, fishing and singing by himself as was his wont. In 1915, he made an automobile trip across the continent to the Panama Exposition. A party of six boys with three cars drove from Detroit by way of the Sante Fe Trail, and returned by the Oregon Trail and the Lincoln Highway. He wrote a vivacious and entertaining account of the sights and of the many adventures and mishaps of the long journey. In July, 1918, he was brevetted an Aviator Pilot of the Aero Club of America.

Aside from such ordinary uneventful incidents of a boy's life and of association with a large family and troops of friends who loved him dearly, there is little to record except the last eventful experiences told in his letters, and the circumstances of his final sacrifice.

He was attached to the 95th Aero Squadron, First Pursuit Group of the American Air Service, and went to the front at one of the most active fighting sectors on July 16th, 1918. He undertook actual service at once as a pursuit pilot over the enemy lines at Château Thierry and was in many battles. The day before his last patrol, he took part in an air combat in which four Boche planes were downed. On the morning of August 11th, 1918, just one year from the day he wrote, "At last I am a regular aviator," when he was the rear guard of a patrol of thirteen Spad, type 13, 220 H. P. planes, and flying very high—higher than the other machines and well behind them—he was cut off by a formation of five German Fokkers which came out of the sun upon him. His companions saw him start fighting, and immediately attacked the enemy planes, but he was separated from them in the dog fight, and they never saw him again.

One of his companions in the air battle writes:

We got two of the Boche planes, but it was dreadfully hard luck

1896

just the same. Bill had fought his last fight, and he was the kind we hate to lose.

It was at the time of the fierce and constant battles near the Vesle River and the only further accounts of his last fight came by telephone message from the 133rd French Infantry which reported that he was seen in combat with a number of enemy planes over the vicinity of Vauxcere, and that, although at a great disadvantage, he was handling his craft with skill and strategy, and had just made a double *renverse*, when he must have been hit and started for his own lines, and very soon the plane, as if without control, glided and crashed to the earth within the Allied lines.

Another account from the same source states that in the midst of the fighting, his plane suddenly fluttered as if it had no driver, and crashed to the ground within the enemy lines, and that on the same day the French made an advance and took the territory where he lay. No more definite information has yet been attainable. On the same day, he was buried by strangers in the grave where he now lies in the Communal Cemetery of the village of Courville, France, about three kilometres south of Fismes. The rude cross marking the spot bears the inscription, carefully and clearly made with a lead pencil—

VILLIAM M. RUSSEL

First Lieutenant

Aviateur Americain

11

Aout

1918.

Long before our country was compelled to intervene, he apparently realised that war was unavoidable, and was inspired with a foresight of the game in life "where what he most would value must be won." His letters clearly exhibit his spirit and feelings and show what steps he had taken before consulting his father, and his satisfaction that his desires and intentions were approved.

The reader will, no doubt, agree that he possessed the characteristics which the poet ascribes, and can truthfully be called a Happy Warrior.

Detroit, Mich.,
January, 1919.

1900

Over Here

Ithaca, New York,
April 1, 1917.

Henry Russel,
917 Jefferson Avenue,
Detroit, Michigan.
War is sure. Maury and I want to enlist. Will you
meet us New York tomorrow and take us to Washington?

William M. Russel.

Telegram

Detroit, Michigan,
April 1, 1917.

William M. Russel,
Kappa Alpha Lodge,
Ithaca, N.Y.
Glad you desire to enlist, but do not be so fast. Can't meet you
tomorrow. If you have not time to write, wire me night letter
telling more about your plans and wishes.

Henry Russel.

Night Letter

Ithaca, New York,
April 2, 1917.

Henry Russel,
Detroit. Thanks for message. Maury and I have already made
application here for enlistment in aviation. If we pass examinations, we go in as privates on promise of lieutenants' commissions if we can pass flying tests after instruction. You can help
to get prompt action. That's all we want. They might string us

along three weeks. Have passed all college exams. University will let us go now to enlist. My degree will come in June.

William.

Telegram

Detroit, Michigan,
April 3, 1917.

William M. Russel,
Ithaca.
Am leaving for New York tomorrow. Can you meet us at Biltmore Thursday? Answer.

Henry Russel.

Telegram

Ithaca, New York,
April 4, 1917.

Henry Russel,
Detroit.
Yes.

William.

At New York, he was taken to the office of one of the great business concerns, and to his surprise, his employment by the company was discussed in his presence. A desirable position, which would have given him the opportunity of foreign travel was offered, and he was told that he could begin work in the New York office the next day. He bowed and said, "Thanks," but nothing more until he was out on Broadway, when he exclaimed, "Father, I can't take that job. I must enlist. Aren't you going to take me to Washington?"

His friend, Maury Hill of St. Louis, Missouri, now a captain in the Air Service, met him in Washington, and on April 14, 1917, the two boys were notified that they had passed their physical and mental examinations, and that certificates of enlistment would be issued, and they returned to Ithaca.

The certificate of enlistment, dated May 10, 1917, states that William M. Russel was enlisted as Sergeant, Aviation Section, Signal Corps, Enlisted Reserve Corps of the Army of the United States on the 26th day of April, 1917, for the period of four years.

Telegram

Washington, D. C,
April 23, 1917.

Sergeant William M. Russel,
Detroit.
Captain Milling has ordered your and Hill's enlistment. Much time will be saved by beating it at your expense, and reporting to officer in charge, Memphis Training Camp. Telegraphic orders will be there. You are an honour to your country. Good luck.

Hutton.

Telegram

Detroit, Michigan,
April 24, 1917.

A. R. Christy,
Captain Signal Corps,
Aviation School,
Memphis, Tenn.
Have advice of enlistment from Washington, and to report to you. Expect to reach Memphis Thursday afternoon, twenty-sixth instant.

William M. Russel.

Telegram

Detroit, Michigan,
April 24, 1917.

Sergeant Maury Hill,
5505 Lindell Blvd.,
St. Louis, Mo.
Telegram from Major Hutton saying our enlistment ordered, and to report at once at Memphis. I will leave here tomorrow, due Memphis Thursday noon. Cordova Hotel.

Bill.

Hotel Chisca,
Memphis, Tennessee,
April 27, 1917.

Dear Father—I have arrived safely after a rather long trip on a very poor train—from Fulton to Memphis on a local.

At Chicago, I found Bill Blair waiting for me at the station, and we drove to the College Inn, where we talked nothing but aviation in particular and in general. He has received his Pilot's license from the Aero Club of America, and now wishes to be in the government service. He expects to go to Washington, and will try to be assigned to

DETROIT UNIVERSITY SCHOOL (D. U. S.) 1906

Memphis to complete his course.

I found Maury at the station when I reached Memphis. Tell Uncle Jere that he has become a back number. The Cordova Hotel, to which he referred me, was torn down years ago. We found this hotel where we are well fixed for the time being, but expect at once to hunt for an apartment or a rooming house.

The field is about eight miles from town, and remote from everything. What do you think of my picking up a cheap second-hand car or a Ford? We have to report at the field every morning at seven o'clock, and it is about three-quarters of an hour's ride on the trolley, and a substantial walk afterwards.

I have already met a good many of the young men in the school, and they are certainly a clean-cut lot of fellows. Captain Christy, the boss, is fine.

At present, there are about thirty aeroplanes here, ten or more being up in the air most of the time.

This will give you a fair notion of what I have done and seen so far. Will let you know my definite address as soon as I get located. In the meantime, write me here. Your loving son,

William.

Memphis, Tennessee,
April 29, 1917.

Dear Father—

We have had a very cordial reception from everybody here, and although we had no letters of introduction, I think we have been fortunate. I had not been here half an hour before I met two very good friends from Cornell, whom I did not even know lived here. They have taken us out for lunch and dinner, and have introduced us to many nice people. Out at the field, too, we have found a fine lot of college fellows.

The instructor to whom I will probably be assigned is a Cornell graduate of 1905, and about as enthusiastic a Cornellian as I have ever met. This afternoon, he will introduce us to all of our superior officers.

On our arrival, we found orders O. K. to enlist us, but not to put us into actual service, so Thursday afternoon, after being sworn in, I was permitted to go into town and wire Major Hutton for the other order. On Friday noon, it came from Washington, and we were immediately put into active service.

Saturday, we reported to Lieutenant Brown for vaccination and ty-

HILL SCHOOL 1912

phoid fever serum injection. The latter made me very ill, and I was at once placed on the sick list. I went to the hotel, slept all the afternoon and night, and ate nothing until this morning. Now, I feel fairly well, although I still have some fever. They tell me it will last some days, and then I will have the second and third injections.

Monday morning, I report to Sergeant Lyle in the repair department at seven o'clock. I don't know how soon I will begin flying.

In regard to the rooming quarters, Maury and I have been on the go every minute we could, trying to find something near the field. The nearest boarding houses are about two miles away, and apartment houses are over in the opposite side of the city, and inconvenient to the car line which runs only every half hour. Joe Galloway has asked us to visit him until we can get settled, but his house is also remote. Mr. Hill has just this minute telephoned me saying that he knows of a good boarding house which will be convenient.

The weather is like mid-summer in Detroit. Flowers and trees are all in bloom, I am glad I brought my summer clothing. We are told that our entire uniform and equipment except leather *puttees* will be furnished.

Hope you are all well.

Your loving son,

William.

N. B.—I was glad to see Jim Buckley for a few minutes yesterday. He is trying hard to get by and enlist, and I hope he will make it.

Wm.

Memphis, Tennessee,
May 1, 1917.

Dear Father—

Work has begun in earnest, and I must admit it is a more novel experience than I expected. We were ordered to report at the field yesterday at seven o'clock, which meant rising at 5:15 in the morning, a hasty breakfast, and a long ride. Dressed in our overalls, we were at once set to strenuous mental and manual labour; taking instruction by lecture, and tearing down and assembling aeroplanes. The work is entirely new to me, and has to be done rapidly, but it is amazing how much one can learn by practical experience even without instruction. At twelve o'clock, a bugle sounds, which informs us that we can check in our tools and rush to a small cafeteria across from the field and stand up to a delicious luncheon of ham and egg sandwiches and

85

a bottle of coca cola. I then crawl into one of the hangars and have a rest—that is, if I rush my sandwich.

Another bugle at one o'clock, and we return to the assembling and repair department. Work then continues until four o'clock, when we are summoned for muster and inspection. At 4:30, we have drill for half an hour; then two or three times a week, a lecture on aero-dynamics, after which we scoot for town and get a good bath and a better dinner. It may seem incredible to you, but I am enjoying work, and outside of a few aching bones, never felt better in my life.

Bob Townes and Joe Galloway have done everything in the world for us.

I had dinner and a good visit with Jim Buckley the other evening. He has failed in his physical exam, for aviation on account of bad eyes. The average down here accepted is five out of twenty-four examined.

You will understand that it will take some little time for me to become accustomed to work, so I will not write you again for a few days.

Love to all.

Your loving son,

William.

Memphis, Tennessee,
May 8, 1917.

Dear Father—

Never before have I looked forward so eagerly to Saturday after-noon and Sunday for rest as now, at the end of the first real working week of my life. I felt, however, that such a breath from Heaven as a week-end rest was too good to be true. Sure enough, it was so. Friday evening, I was summoned to headquarters and ordered to report for guard duty at twelve o'clock Sunday, and had to pace the field until six o'clock—then off until eight o'clock, when I was again on guard until ten, then off until two a. m., when I went on guard again until four o'clock Monday morning. I was fortunate in not encountering any spies or plotters, although I was armed to the teeth. The next night, the watch, who was on guard for the same hours to which I was as-signed, brought in a suspect who is now under arrest.

My work during each day has been practically the same. To prove how strenuous, it is, it will probably surprise you to know that I have been in bed every night by a quarter of nine, with the exception of Sunday night guard duty. I have, however, been placed on the flying

CORNELL UNIVERSITY 1915

list, which means that I have a flight every day, weather permitting. My first ride was what they call a joy ride. You merely sit and endeavour to accustom yourself to the new sensations.

From now on, I will be permitted to drive with the instructor at another set of controls behind me to correct any fault. It is hard to describe the feeling. At first it gives you very peculiar sensations in your stomach and ears. One thing that surprised me was the roughness of the riding. Looking at an aeroplane from the ground, it seems to glide, but the riding in the aeroplanes in use here is very rough and choppy. It may be a consolation to you to know that I have been assigned to an instructor who is said to be the most conservative flyer on the field.

We were told today that this field had been condemned because it was too small, and that the detachment would either be moved to Indianapolis or Chicago. I am not sure of this, but it is positive that we will move somewhere within the next month.

I received your letter from Detroit, but failed to get either the letter or the paper from New York. I was exceedingly sorry to hear about the death of Gus Porter, and regret that the newspaper giving the details did not come. He was one of the bravest, best fellows ever, and it is hard that he has been taken so soon. I heard, also, that Charlie Weigonel, another of my good friends at Cornell, was killed in an accident at Newport. He was in training for the torpedo chasers, the mosquito fleet.

I have purchased, for a hundred dollars, a second-hand Hupmobile which will run, and am now operating a free jitney.

Tonight, I am dining with Joe Galloway at his father's beautiful residence in Memphis, and on Sunday, will have dinner with Mr. Lee, a friend of Maury's father.

The trout reels are all in the top drawer of the table in my room on the third floor.

What do you hear from our good old fishing friend Walter Brackett, of the Ste. Marguerite? Is he a hundred years old yet?

Love to all,

Your loving son,

William.

★★★★★★

Walter M. Brackett, the celebrated painter and salmon fisherman of Boston, died before this book was completed, on March 4, 1919, at the age of 96 years.

★★★★★★

Memphis, Tennessee,
May 10, 1917.

Dear Father—

This noon, I had my second inoculation for typhoid, and have again been placed on the sick list. The doctor told me to keep out of the sun, and not to take any exercise. As yet, however, I feel fine, with no signs of fever.

Next week has a good deal in store for us in the way of work. Yesterday, orders came from Washington that all further flying on this field should cease, as it is too small to be safe. Captain Royce immediately notified us, and then rumours were rife. Some were sure that we would leave immediately for Indianapolis; some. Mobile; some, San Antonio; and others, Chicago. I think the chances are, we will be sent to Chicago. Tomorrow, we start packing the aeroplanes and camp equipment. This will take us about a week, and then I suppose we will be informed of our destination.

If Chicago is selected, we will probably be placed in barracks as soon as they can be constructed. My flying was advancing rapidly up to the time when this change was ordered. I am afraid my next flight will be far in the future.

I had a very fine letter from Christine from New York, and also from Allen, giving me the names of several of his Memphis friends. Have received the book, *Military Aeroplanes*. It is a good technical book, and I am studying it with interest.

I hope you are all well.

Your loving son,

William.

This letter encloses a newspaper clipping, dated Paris, May 9, 1917, as follows:

The Stars and Stripes appeared on the streets of Paris as the battle flag of an armed force this morning, when the flag and fifty men of the American Field Service under it on their way to the railway station for the front were acclaimed enthusiastically by early risers all along the route. Thirty-one members of the contingent are from Cornell University. This is the first detachment of the American Field Service to bear arms, and is detailed for the transportation of munitions to the front.

Memphis, Tennessee,
May 11, 1917.

Dear Father—

My second inoculation for typhoid yesterday gave me no fever. I returned to my room, waiting all afternoon for evil effects to come, but instead of that, I felt better and better. This morning, I wakened at the usual early hour, and felt so good that I did not take the rest of my 24-hour leave, and reported to the field. It was a mistake, because I found about the busiest day of my short enlistment experience awaiting me. Two other men and myself tore down two entire machines and packed them for shipment.

It is announced that we will go to Ashburn, near Chicago. We do not know definitely whether we are to find our own quarters or live in barracks (tents) there. Whatever the quarters may be, the change will be welcome. It is terribly hot and uncomfortable here, and, of course, we will have a larger and less dangerous field. It will, however, hold back our training some three weeks. The next few days will surely be busy ones with all the tearing down and packing that must be done.

Sunday, Maury and I, as I wrote you, expect to dine with Mr. and Mrs. Robert Lee.

One young fellow came here, entered the aviation school, and about a week after his arrival, was thrown into the guard house. He is suspected of being pro-German, and although he has now been under guard for several weeks, there is no indication of a trial set for him yet.

Another boy has also been placed under guard, and removed from the flying list because he cheated in an examination. Although he is still in the camp, he will probably be dishonourably discharged. Captain Royce gave us a good talk on this subject yesterday, and told us the way it was dealt with at West Point.

I have the New York papers which you sent, and note that the government has refused to recognise the Yale Battery as an army unit.

I will probably now be able to see you soon.

With love to all,

William.

Memphis, Tennessee,
May 13, 1917.

Dear Father—

There is a general supposition that the easiest and quickest way to obtain a commission in the reserve army is in aviation. This, I can assure you, is wholly erroneous, and whenever you hear it repeated, you can deny it with authority of sixty-nine young fellows down here. My experience is just the same as the others. I have been here a little over two weeks, and have not had an afternoon or morning off except the sick absences following the inoculations required in the army regulations. Both Saturdays and Sundays have been spent at the field. I have just now returned from my usual seven a. m. to four p. m. hours. Of course, Sunday work is not ordinary, but if it happens to suit the captain's fancy, or there is something unusual, there is no alternative, and no extra pay, and no less danger, although we never think of that.

Everything is being pushed to make the earliest departure possible for Ashburn, near Chicago. We will leave Wednesday if the cars for the transportation of our material can be had. We are told that we will have two days at Chicago to obtain quarters until barracks can be built.

Maury and I and two other boys are considering Hotel Windermere, which is very convenient to the field, although seven miles away. There is fair train service to and from the field. Here, we have a plot of ground about the size of a large city block on which to descend. In Chicago, the field is more than a mile square, with open surrounding country on which forced landings can be made. This change has caused more delay in our flying. No machines have ascended since last Tuesday, and it will probably be at least two weeks before any more flights will be made.

In comparison with an automobile, it has been surprising to me how simple the construction of an aeroplane is, and the rapidity with which it can be set up and torn down. To enable us to become familiar with the construction of an aeroplane, this move has been a God-send to us, as we are learning it at first hand in detail in the most practical way.

Allen's friend, Mr. Maury, came out to the field to see me the other day, and he could not have arrived at a more inopportune time. I was in overalls, and as black as the Jack of Spades. It was a curious coincidence that he is Maury's cousin, and they had not seen or known each other before. He was very kind, and offered to give us every sort of diversion, but it is all in vain. We have not a minute off. By the time I am cleaned up in the evening, it is dinner time, and bed time follows immediately. Sundays are our only chance, and so far, I have been deprived of both.

Our visit here has been very good, and Memphis is an attractive city. The people seem to me to be like those of Los Angeles. The weather is so regular, and much of the time so hot, that they are easy going. There is none of the hustle and bustle to which I have been accustomed. You can observe it on the streets as well as in conversation. They have the slow Southern drawl which impresses me as a waste of time. I will feel more at home in Chicago. We will locate Bill Blair there, and he will surely help us out. Hoping to see you in Chicago, I am.

      With love,

                                         William.

Telegram

                                   Chicago, Ill.,
                                 May 21, 1917.

Henry Russel,
Detroit.
Arrived Chicago after tiresome thirty-two-hour trip from Memphis. At Hotel Fort Dearborn. Week of hard work before machines are set up and flying resumed. Ashburn is very desolate, but the field and surroundings seem fine. Well.
Love.   W. M. R.

                                   Chicago, Ill.,
                                 May 23, 1917.

Dear Father—
This is the first chance I have had to write. The loading continued last week up to the last minute, and then I received the unpleasant news to report at once for guard duty. The loaded freight cars were pulled out into the yard in a remote part of the city, and four of us were ordered to stand guard over the train all night. We worked in three shifts.

My hours were ten to twelve and two to four. After that, until train time, we were all on guard. It was very unpleasant work owing to the nasty location.

The train left at eleven, and then began an awful railroad trip. Our first stop was at a lonely little town about five in the afternoon, where we ate a poor luncheon and supper combined. There were no more stops that evening, and the next day, we made an untimely stop for an equally bad breakfast about ten o'clock. The third stop, about four in the afternoon, gave us our lunch. At six o'clock, we arrived in

Chicago, and apparently were not expected. It was a good thing I had drawn that draft on you in Memphis and had some money, because we had to pay for our train fare and meals, but were told that it would be credited to our accounts.

We have not received a cent of pay yet, and expenses have been heavy. My only extravagance so far has been that hundred-dollar automobile. The man I bought it of feels confident that I can sell it and get my money back.

On arrival at Chicago, we went to the Fort Dearborn Hotel because it was most convenient. Orders were given out the night of our arrival to report at the field next morning at seven o'clock sharp.

Ashburn is located fourteen miles out of Chicago in a most desolate place. It is simply a railroad junction with two or three small dwellings in the neighbourhood. There are four trains a day, the first leaving at six o'clock a. m.—our train. We reported according to orders, and in a nasty cold rain. It was such a contrast to Memphis that everybody took cold. There were no warehouses or sheds, and we had to unload the planes on the ground in the open, and then carry or push them nearly a mile. When lunch time came, we were let off for an hour, but there was no place to eat.

We finally managed to get some crackers, no cheese or anything else, and nothing hot. All this rush was deemed necessary because the orders were to save demurrage on the cars. The next day, we had the same experience, but were finally rescued from the two regular army sergeants in charge by the captain, who ordered them to stop the nonsense, and to let the planes remain in the cars, protected from the elements until a storage place could be found, and to let us go to get some clothing suitable to the climate and to find permanent quarters. This morning, we were required to report to the field again as usual, but were allowed to go at once.

We have found the Drexel Arms not luxurious, but very good. There are five of us together—two boys from Nashville, one from St. Louis, one from Indianapolis, and one from a city which I am afraid I never really appreciated before.

I do not believe many more hardships can come to us here, and we understand our first pay will come on the 15th of June. Pay checks will be a novel sight to many of us.

Your loving son,

William.

Telegram

Chicago, Ill.,
May 29, 1918.

Henry Russel,
Detroit.
Am not lonely, but would enjoy a visit from you Sunday. Permanent address—Elms Hotel Annex. Answer.

William.

Ashburn, Ill.,
J une 13, 1917.

Dear Father—

The trip home was a delight to me. It was so good to see you all, even for a few hours. The ride back on Sunday afternoon was so different from what I have been accustomed to recently, and the time passed quickly. I was at 53rd Street, Chicago, almost before I knew it, and tucked away in bed by 9 :30 for the early start next morning.

The last two days have been beautiful—the air clear and still. Ten to fifteen machines have been in flight nearly all the time. You cannot imagine the difference between flying at Memphis and here.

At Memphis, we had a small field with heavy woods on one side, where naturally the air was cool and descending rapidly, while on the other side was a lumber yard, on which the sun beat down heating the air, and causing it to rise. On a field of this kind, you can imagine the bumps you hit as you cross from the ascending air into the still air, and then into the descending air. On the other hand, the field here at Ashburn is a mile square, and the surrounding country open, and of the same level, which causes the ride to be a gliding motion, perfectly smooth.

Yesterday, six new machines arrived, the first of a bunch of eighteen which have been ordered for this field, making forty-eight in all. They are standard aeroplanes, manufactured, I think, in Plainfield, New Jersey. The same type of machine is used at Mineola.

Last night, I was again on guard, and after two such perfect days, I thought I was lucky, but the tables turned against me, and the weather went to the worst extreme. All night long, the rain poured down, and the wind whistled around the canvas hangars, and all night long, we paced to and fro. Every half hour, we had to go the rounds with the watchman's clock, and punch it at the different posts. At the end of our guard, we adjourned to headquarters for a four-hour snooze, but found that the blankets and cots had been locked up in the Quartermaster's Department, and as it took a sudden shift from rain to very cold weather, we had to stand shivering in our wet clothes until relieved about six o'clock. Then I went to a farmer's house, and after much pleading, persuaded the good wife to make some coffee for me and let me dry out at her kitchen fire. I am writing to you now from this house.

The papers of the last few days look as if Washington is beginning to take more notice of this branch of the service. There is a bill before Congress to raise the appropriation from seventy to five hundred million, and to establish an aviation portfolio in the Cabinet.

I have been transferred from my former instructor, Mr. Macauley, to Mr. Pond, a son of Admiral Pond. I understand he is quite good, but a different style of flyer from Mr. Macauley. I am sorry to part from Mr. Macauley but think I will like Mr. Pond. At any rate, I am going to stick to orders. It is foolish to ask for a transfer after you have been assigned.

I do not know whether this letter will reach you before you leave for the Little Pabos River. I envy you; at the same time, I would not leave my work here even to go there. I hope you will have as great success as we had last year. Was it not wonderful fishing? Being deprived of a visit to Fontinalis, which I do not think I have ever missed in any year, will be one of the many sacrifices I will now have to make.

I hope you are all well and that every minute of your trip will be pleasant.

Your loving son,

William.

Fourth Aerial Squadron,
Ashburn, Ill.,
June 18, 1917.

Dear Father—

Work has been progressing, although slowly. Since our bad storm the other evening, the weather has been better, and the ground is drying out very rapidly for such a marshy place. The machines are being set up, and by the end of the week, we ought to have all forty-eight in commission. The new machines show beautiful workmanship, but as yet we have had none of them in the air. Some of these machines, we expect, will be equipped with the new "stick" military work I am performing here, no one would think that I was even an imitation of

Aquarium Pool, Little Pabos River

a Bachelor of Arts. I do not realise it myself.

Bill Blair has received his commission as ensign in the United States Naval Aviation Section. He started a school for training men, and now has ten students. He desires to get twenty, and have two or three machines. He telephoned me the other evening, and asked me to learn whether any Detroit men would care to enter this branch and receive a commission after they pass the tests of the Aviation Club of America, and get pilots' licenses. The medical examinations are not severe, and the tests are quite simple. I wired Pat Wardwell all the information, and asked him to post it in the University Club of Detroit. It is really a good opportunity. In that service, nothing is required but straight flying.

On Saturday I went to the Blackstone Hotel for a treat, and ran into a bunch of Detroit people, among others, Charlie Hodges, Tom Whitehead and Edsel Ford. Charlie is at Fort Sheridan. Eddie is full of enthusiasm to enlist, and will probably go into the motor transportation service, or, as he says, drive a car for an officer, if necessary. He will make a millionaire chauffeur. Tom has not made up his mind yet what branch he will take.

I can picture you now, sitting on the banks of the lovely Little Pabos River, looking down into the pool at your feet where those big salmon are. Oh, if I could only follow this letter to its destination! I have, however, the memory of my one trip there, and I take consolation from that, as well as from the hope someday to see and hear the tumbling waters again. Be sure and let me know how the salmon are running and what records are shattered. Goodbye, with love,

William.

Fourth Aerial Squadron,
Ashburn, Ill.,
June 22, 1917.

Dear Father—

The last week has been so perfect, and so much has been accomplished, that I feel as if I had a new lease of life, and am more enthusiastic about flying than ever.

The sun has shone all week, and, as a result, the ground has thoroughly dried out. Last Monday, I made only one flight, but on each of the remaining days, I have made two. With this long consecutive run, I have at last got some confidence in myself, and yet, at the same time, I feel how little I really know. The flying in mid-air above an altitude of two thousand feet is comparatively simple. The quicker action and decision is required as you get nearer the ground. I should say that, barring such accidents to an aeroplane as might happen to an automobile, a locomotive, or even a carriage, from a concealed defect, or the breaking of a part, a fellow is safe when flying at a height of more than one thousand feet; between one thousand and five hundred feet, he is reasonably safe; at less than five hundred feet, there are elements of danger.

You cannot rest even in a straight course as with an automobile. Each little puff of wind swings you to the right or to the left. The early morning flight, however, is very different. The air usually is perfectly quiet, and you glide along like a bird. My instruction last week consisted practically of straight flying, with occasional turns. The early part of this week, I spent in making left hand turns in the form of a circle or square. On Wednesday, I began on right hand turns, which are very different from the left hand ones. This is due to the revolving of the propeller, the tendency being not only to turn your machine to the left, but also to upset it laterally to the left. This must be prevented by giving it right rudder and right aileron more than left, thus holding your machine in a stable position. Seven machines have been somewhat damaged this week on account of too steep a descent before landing. The ground is still somewhat soft, and the front wheels stick in the mud, which throws the tail up in the air, and causes the machine to stand on its nose, and smash the propeller.

Ordinarily, it is not very serious, but rather a nuisance, as it puts the machine out of commission for some time. Aeroplanes now are plentiful. We have forty-eight for the use of seventy-three students. One of our most advanced men, who was already recommended for his commission, has been indefinitely suspended for looping the loop with a passenger. In the first place, it is strictly against the rules for a student to loop the loop without permission of the commanding officer, and secondly, it is forbidden except for an instructor ever to loop with a passenger.

My admiration for the Red Cross has been decidedly increased in the last few days. After having joined in Detroit, Ithaca, Memphis, and Chicago, I am now beginning to reap the reward. It seemed to me it was giving to something that was all right, but vague and far away. Now, I have found it right at home. They have established a Red Cross restaurant on the field, where hot and wholesome food can be had. You cannot imagine what a God-send it is to us. Although we have been able to get coffee, no other form of hot stuff could be had. Now, we get coffee, pork chops, eggs, frankfurters and hamburgers, clean cooked and served. Once a week, too, the best girls of Chicago wait on the table. The rest of the time, we just grab.

I had a fine visit from Pat the other day. I was bending busily over a machine and doing a mechanic's work, when I heard his familiar voice. It was not a very interesting day, as the advanced men were all off on a cross-country flight to Joliet. However, I could show him six or seven machines in sight in the air.

We have word from Captain Royce that he is safe in France. He is the head of the first American Aerial Squadron to be sent to the front—we understand that the American Esquadrille was the first to carry the flag. He is stationed near Paris. He is a fine officer, and I believe we will hear great things of him. Our other commanding officer. Captain Christy, will be married next Saturday, and I am afraid we will lose him.

At last the government has done something real for our branch of the service. Yesterday, the President endorsed the plan of making a $600,000,000.00 appropriation, and we are interested and wondering whether the bill to create a Cabinet member for aviation will pass.

You cannot imagine how much better I have been satisfied since your letter came stating so fully your feelings with respect to this branch of the service. It is a delight to know your attitude, and it will be an inspiration to me. I feel sure that it is a most important branch of war service, and under the new conditions, will be the great factor in bringing this conflict to a close in favour of the Allies; but we must act before it is too late.

The news from the English front is again encouraging. It cannot be that the Russian people will be fooled by the German peace move. On the other hand, it is ominous that the submarine danger is again critical. I note that last week was the worst week yet from this menace.

Mes compliments to the boys, my French-Canadian friends. Good luck.

Your loving son,

William.

Fourth Aerial Squadron,
Ashburn, Ill.,
June 24, 1917.

Dear Father—
Saturday ended by far the best week yet of my training. The good

weather brought new life to everybody. We now have practically all of the planes set up and in. running order. In addition to our forty-eight machines, there are six private aeroplanes. I have been able to get eleven flights since last Monday, and in that many one can accomplish a good deal. I have become perfectly accustomed to the new and rather pleasant sensations, and yet the various flying movements seem as strange and unnatural as ever. On this account, I sometimes feel discouraged, but they tell me the faculty comes to you over night. At any rate I am pinning my faith on this.

The landings still look impossible to me, but as I have not tried to make any yet, it is no wonder.

Saturday night was my turn on guard again, and it was nasty as usual. It is very cold, and no provision made for comfort. Last night two other boys and myself found three blankets and a couple of cots which we set up in headquarters. Only one had to be on guard, so the other two slept. Headquarters, however, is a galvanized steel building, which seems to lower its temperature a lap ahead of the weather. Early in the evening, it was comfortable. Towards morning it became unbearable. We left it and resorted to a bonfire about four in the morning, and slept no more. The cold wind murdered sleep.

At six o'clock we woke up our new faithful Red Cross chef and demanded hot coffee. We told him it was a medicinal necessity to ward off an attack of grippe. I do not quite understand why we have to take this taste of the hardship of warfare. It is a duty performed by the infantry when the real time comes, but I suppose that our branch of the service must be fit to do any military work required, and that is the spirit in which we are fitting ourselves. Just now, if a fixed camp were established here, and barracks built, there would be a company of regulars quartered with us who would relieve us of a great deal of this disagreeable work, and give us more time to fly. Big changes in this respect, we understand, may be made within the next two weeks.

We have had an interesting case of discipline. A regular private was ordered to guard duty to fill the place of a reserve who had been excused by a petty officer. This, we are told, is against army regulations, as only the commanding officer can excuse a man. The private, therefore, refused to stand guard, and talked back to the petty officer. He was thereupon reported and court-martialled for refusing to do guard duty and insulting a superior officer. On being called to headquarters, he declined the summary court, and demanded general court-martial. The regulars think the man is a martyr, and that there is discrimination in favour of the reserves. While there is little chance of saving this private, they hope to get the post upon a more strictly military basis, where such discrimination cannot occur. To a certain group of the reserves, this will come as a hard blow, because some of them have been favoured. My sympathy is entirely with the regulars, and I hope they will be successful. Some of the officers have apparently punched a hole in a hornet's nest.

Your fine box of fruit came today, with enough good things in it to support a large camping party for a week. My digestion is surely all right. After a hard, dirty day, two of us tonight took a bath, and then climbed at once into bed and ate a couple of melons and a liberal supply of cheese sandwiches, and felt the better for it. The cheese tasted like the fine one we had on the Petit Pabos. How we used to gouge out chunks after each meal and wash them down with Mr. Davis's champagne cider, which he used to claim was just as good as champagne, even if he never got anybody to agree with him.

We have no recreation here. In the evening, on returning from the field, we stop in a little cafeteria and have a light supper (it is not *en regle* to wash), then straight to bed. We have to rise at 4:45 every morning except Sunday in order to make train connections, and answer roll call at 7:15 at the hangars, which are a mile and a quarter from the station.

A taste of the Petit Pabos salmon would be appetising if you will send one to this bunch of flyers. I am sure they would cook it for us right at our hotel. The chef has been very obliging.

Thanks once more for the overflowing box, and if you send another, will thank you again.

Good luck, *bon fortune, au revoir*. Regards to Francois and the other boys.

Your loving son,

William.

Fourth Aerial Squadron,
Ashburn, Ill.,
June 29, 1917.

Dear Father—

The delightful weather of last week did not last. This week it has gone to the other extreme. Monday was the only day I could make a flight. The rest of the time the rain has beaten down, and the field is practically lost to the eye under four inches of water.

Shortly after my flight Monday, all flying was stopped on account of a nasty accident to one of the solo men, who escaped miraculously from a wreck in a tail spin. This is a form of accident which a novice aviator must always guard against. It is usually the result of carelessness or a moment's forgetfulness. From the minute you first begin instruction, you are warned about it, and told how to keep out of it. A "tail spin," as it is called, is caused from losing headway. It results from two factors—failing to nose the machine down on the turns, and failing to keep the direction of the wind clearly in mind. On making a turn, if you do not nose the machine towards the ground, you necessarily lose such headway that the plane becomes uncontrollable.

The nose will drop on account of the weight of the motor, throwing the tail into the air. If the wind is coming from a side direction, it will strike the plane, whirling the tail, and tend to spin it around the nose as an axis. Your only chance to gain control is to head to the ground with the motor off and the rudder held against the wind until you gain sufficient headway to get control once more of the machine. If you are at an altitude of over five hundred feet, your safety is assured, otherwise a wreck is imminent. This boy kept his head remarkably well, and never ceased fighting to gain control.

When they got him out of the wreckage with only a couple of minor cuts on his face and a bad shaking up, they went over every part of his machine. It was badly smashed, but the controls were all in good condition. He fell about two hundred feet, and in that small space of time he had removed his glass goggles, unfastened his safety-belt, throttled the motor, and shut off the spark—the four things he should have done. As I said, after this accident, all flying was called off for the rest of that day, and for the remainder of the week, it has poured rain.

Another rather unfortunate experience of a different kind has come to one of the boys, a nice fellow, this week. He entered just about the time I did, and it has been evident that flying did not appeal to him. All the time he struggled to overcome his aversion to the new sensations, but somehow, they were so unnatural to him that he failed to master his feelings. Wednesday, he went with tears in his eyes to headquarters, and after a long talk with the captain, was released from the Aviation Corps. He was a brave enough fellow, and wanted to continue. This is the second case we have had. It seems that one's feelings are not controllable. You are either fascinated or dread it.

Rumours are rife again that we are about to move to Rantoul, Illinois. No further word has been given out, but I think there is little doubt but that we will go within the next two or three weeks. If we do go there, we will have a taste of real army life, because it is an established army post, and we will live in barracks under strict military discipline. The flying field, near a village of about a thousand people, is practically finished. The ground is well drained, and the hangars and barracks, I understand, are already constructed.

Tomorrow, we will have inspection here by a board of officers from Washington. Several members of the Royal Flying Corps of England and France will accompany them.

During this rainy spell, all the planes have been put in good running condition, and the extra time consumed in putting a polish on, I suppose that you have heard that the Curtis Aeroplane Company has been reorganised and new equipment has been installed so that it is said they can make five thousand machines this year.

The increase in the appropriation for aviation has received the O. K. of the President and the Secretaries of War and the Navy, and I take it will now be favourably acted upon by Congress. I suppose the War and Navy Departments will not favour a separate Cabinet officer for aviation. It is such a novel and distinct branch of the service, and will play such a part in the determination of the war that I think its separate control will be adopted before the end.

I have a postal card from Eleanor today, saying that the news from you was fifty salmon for the party in two days. This sounds as though last year with our great record may be a lean year in comparison.

I am more and more interested in my work here, and would not change now to any other work or recreation, but I must admit that stories from the Little Pabos give me a longing. I am there with you in thought, and wish you good luck and a good rest. Write me all about it.

> Your loving son,
>
> William.

> Fourth Aerial Squadron,
> Ashburn, Ill.,
> July 5, 1917.

Dear Father—

I have just come back from the field after another cold night of guard duty. I hope it will be the last here.

Saturday, we leave for Rantoul, where we will be stationed in newly built barracks, and will have a company of infantry attached. Instead of wasting the time getting to and from the field, we will have the advantage of practicing in the still air of the mornings and evenings. It will give us three hours more of flying each day. Captain Spain and one of our flying instructors flew over there yesterday to make arrangements for us. It is a trip of one hundred and ten miles, and the journey each way was made in about an hour and a half. They say that there is no better flying field in the country. A concrete foundation, covering about forty acres, has been laid so that we will not have the trouble and danger of either starting or landing on the wet, soggy ground.

Saturday noon, thirty-eight machines, each carrying two passengers, will rise at short intervals and fly to Rantoul in a line. It will be a novel movement in American army experience to transport a corps in this way. I think I will be permitted to be a passenger in one of the planes, Mr. Pond's, and if so, he will probably let me drive it all the way down. This will be considered extra time, and not marked against my instruction hours. The other ten machines will be torn down and shipped by freight.

Barracks life will be new to me, but I feel sure it will be preferable to the haphazard way we have been living. It will save an hour or two's time in the morning, and instead of grabbing breakfast and rushing to a train, we can have a snappy setting up exercise and a peaceful breakfast afterwards, and so much the more flying; lunch at 11:30—a thing we have not known here—will be served; one o'clock another roll call; two o'clock, an hour of drill; three to five, recitations in aero-dynamics, practical electricity, and meteorology; five to seven, two more hours of flying instead of a tramp or run to the junction and a ride on a freight train, and a scramble on a crowded trolley car—then supper and bunk (I mean bed, of course).

Everything will be orderly and systematic under strict discipline. A new commanding officer, Captain Brown, I understand, will be in charge of the post, with three French aviation officers, who have just come over from the front. I had the good fortune to go in with them from the field today—Lieutenants Gauthier, Laffly and La Pier. The latter, I am told, has twenty-eight German planes to his credit. They will conduct the courses in military science of the air. One of the many interesting things I learned was that their fighting machines can travel at a speed of one hundred and fifty miles an hour, with a landing speed of ninety miles an hour.

Contrast this with our maximum flying speed of eighty miles and a landing speed of forty miles. You will appreciate how little we will really know, even after we have received our complete instruction on this side. He told me, too, about Guynemer, the great aviator who has forty-nine German machines to his credit. He said that Guynemer, as an aviator, was only a mediocre flyer, and that his great success lay in his daring and remarkable marksmanship, often bringing down the enemy plane with one shot.

Speaking about life over there, he said we would probably be quartered in some *château* or barracks, and be taken to and from the field in an automobile. Our fighting for the day would consist of two flights each morning and evening, except when specific orders were given to carry out reconnaissance work, or a bombing raid. It has been their custom, if one was fortunate enough to bring down an enemy plane, to allow a three days' leave. So far, the action of single planes has been left to the discretion of each aviator in fighting. Your own fancy and wish dictates. All this will, no doubt, soon be changed.

Aunt Jennie has sent me a fine air pillow, enclosed in a light pigskin case, with my initials on it. It will be very convenient. I have never seen anything like it. It came from Cousin Anne Hendrie from London.

It was very thoughtful of Colonel Littebrant to write from Honolulu inviting me to join his Artillery unit, but please say to him that I am in aviation, and have not the slightest desire to retrace my steps. This is the life!

If you have not already sent the salmon to me, do not do so. Send it to some married man who is keeping house. It is not convenient food for a single man in barracks.

My next letter will be from Chanute Field, Rantoul.

May the good luck keep up.

Your loving son,

William.

Chanute Field, Rantoul, Ill.,
July 13, 1917.

Dear Father—

After working from seven until five on Saturday and Sunday, we left for Rantoul at ten o'clock Monday morning. The aeroplanes started at five o'clock a. m. To my great disappointment, I did not get a chance to fly. It was a wonderful sight to watch the departure of the machines as they rose from the field at the early sunrise hour. One at a time, they circled their way up to an altitude of three thousand feet, and in a V formation, two minutes apart, struck south, following the Illinois Central tracks. The first machine covered the distance of one hundred and fourteen miles in eighty-six minutes, and the remaining machines dropped into the field at Rantoul within thirty-five minutes after the first. The entire trip was made without a single mishap with the exception of one machine, which was forced to land in Paxton for more gasoline. The aviator descended safely, replenished his supply, and covered the remaining distance without trouble.

On account of the method of assignment, I missed my chance to ride. The instructors were first chosen as drivers. The solo men took the remaining planes, either as drivers or passenger mechanics—then the civilian mechanics filled the remaining cars. Practically all the students were left out.

My journey to Rantoul, however, was almost as great an experience, lacking the element of excitement. As I said, we were already to leave, with everything packed, and every man reported at ten o'clock sharp. At eleven o'clock the train pulled out in a rather hesitating way, and five hours later we were exactly nine miles away with empty stomachs. To encourage us, Sergeant Moore announced that at Kankakee, fifty miles away, we would stop fifteen minutes for refreshments. At 7:30 the train pulled into this Indian village, and you can imagine the scene when one hundred and fifty hungry fellows rushed into the small restaurant and demanded a combination lunch and dinner served in fifteen minutes. We ate, those of us who could get anything, whatever we could grab.

It was eleven o'clock when we arrived at Rantoul, and there a real reception was tendered. The entire town, some eleven hundred people, was at the station to welcome us with flags and a brass band. They seemed disappointed when the small and dirty troop alighted. We stood at attention with our suitcases for side arms, and a tired, disheartened bunch marched to the field, about three-quarters of a mile away, and crowded into the barracks to have the first taste of army life. None was disappointed. We entered a large room, which presumably would hold about seventy-five cots. It was equipped with about thirty, and fifteen blankets.

I was among those who had neither, and we curled up in the corner on the floor. The day had been unbearably hot, but towards evening it turned colder and colder, until midnight, when it became almost frigid. The morning was very welcome, and hungry and cold, we reported at reveille to find that we had to hunt breakfast where we could get it, and report back to unload the cars at 7:15.

Fortunately, the Tenth Aerial Squadron had arrived several days before from San Antonio, Texas, and after our hasty breakfast, they helped us to unload the machinery and supplies. From now on, they will be our helpers, and new squadrons will be formed from our two. A squadron in aviation consists of one hundred and fifty men and twelve aviators. Our squadron will supply the aviators, and the Tenth will supply mechanics, guards and orderlies. They are fine, clean-cut, big fellows, and have been in training on the border for ten months. We thought at first the feeling would be rather strained, because they are subordinate to us, but all is fair weather when good fellows get together. Another bit of good news was that a company of militia is stationed at the post.

To tell you something of the location and the barracks—the field is situated on the edge of a small town, about fourteen miles from Champaign, in the levelest of level country. For the purpose of a flying field, it cannot be surpassed, and although not quite complete, is in good condition for use. Seventeen hundred men have been working on it for seven weeks. On one side is a row of huge wooden hangars, each with a capacity of six aeroplanes. Behind the hangars is a row of sixteen very good new barracks, each with a good bathroom and shower. Behind the barracks are the mess halls still under construction, and next the officers' quarters. Scattered about are other buildings for Headquarters, Y. M. C. A., motor house, and repair houses. Excellent roads and paths wind in and out among the buildings, and the grounds beyond have been laid out.

The buildings are all white, and mark the field from a long distance. It is an ideal location for concentrated instruction and flying, and we will have far more flying hours than before. Seventy-two machines are expected within three weeks. I think we will be able to have instruction in any kind of weather.

Eight of the more advanced students will get their commissions next week.

Our days here will be as thoroughly occupied as before, and to a greater advantage. At present the order is reveille at six o'clock, breakfast at 6:30, roll call at 7:15, and work until lunch, 11:30; at one o'clock, another roll call, and work, lectures, and flying until 5:30; supper at 5:45; retreat at seven o'clock, and the ending of a perfect day at ten o'clock, when lights are out. When we are comfortably settled with beds and blankets, and the mess hall is finished, all will be well, and it will be as good and healthy a life as one can wish for. This will give you a notion of what my first military existence is. It is rumoured that we are the last reserves in this corps, and that we will be transferred into the regulars when we receive our commissions.

Your letters from the Petit Pabos sound better than ever—and I would almost trade my experience for two weeks in camp with you. You certainly have had wonderful fishing. Do not think that I am having a hard life. I am happy and contented, and the thought of the service aviators can render keeps me cheerful. A fellow cannot help, however, but envy you on that Canadian stream, and after it on the sea shore at Cape Cod.

Hoping I will be able to visit you there before the summer is over, I am,

Your loving son,

William.

Fourth Aerial Squadron,
Rantoul, Illinois,
July 15, 1917.

Dear Cousin Anne—

It was a pleasant surprise when your nice pillow from London was forwarded to me by Aunt Jennie, and I cannot express my appreciation enough for your remembrance. It will be most convenient in barracks where one is fortunate even to have a cot and blankets in our unsettled and unfinished condition.

You can readily imagine that the declaration of war by the United States was not unexpected, and some time before Christmas, I began preparing for it in a very quiet way. On returning to college after Christmas, I arranged with the faculty of the University in regard to my degree, which would, in the ordinary course, only have been given at graduation in June. When I was assured that it would be given in my absence, I filed an application with the Aviation Section of the Officers Signal Reserve Corps. Having done this, the most difficult part of the task lay before me, namely, gaining the permission of father to enter the Aviation Service.

Easter brought the entry of the United States into the war, and moments of anxiety came. At this time, father met me in New York, and I laid before him my plans and told him then, for the first time, what I had done. He hesitated for only a few minutes—the news seemed to strike him like a blow—but he answered as one would expect, that it was a grave problem, and every boy who was fit should decide for himself. My mind was set, and that evening we went to Washington, where the necessary examinations were passed, and I was enlisted. I returned to college for two days, and then went by way of Detroit directly to Memphis, Tennessee, where my aviation training started, on April 26.

You may be interested in our methods of training. You are set directly to flying after the first day, when you ascend for a ride to accustom yourself to the new sensations. This is called the "joy ride." From then on, unless there is some natural defect or personal characteristic which prevents, the controls are given over to you, and you drive the machine under the guidance and aid of another set of controls operated from the rear seat. On becoming more proficient, you are put in the rear seat, and later you are sent up alone to do solo work. After twenty hours of solo work, you are allowed to undertake your flying tests for a commission. Then you are sent to France or England to have another month of instruction on high-powered machines. I am just about to be turned loose; that is, to begin solo work. If we have good flying weather, it will require about five weeks more training in this country.

Our day's work is well laid out for us, and we have little time for recreation. We rise at 5:45 in the morning, have a good setting-up exercise, and a fair breakfast, then we are set directly to work with the machine crew. Six fellows have charge of the upkeep of two machines. When your turn to make a flight comes, an orderly notifies you, and you take half an hour in the air. At eleven and twelve o'clock you report for classes in aero-dynamics and practical electricity. Noon mess is usually a light meal. In the afternoon, we have military drill, class in meteorology, and the remaining time in the motor room where we tear down and assemble motors. The evening is usually spent in study, preparing for the final examinations by which our commissions will be ranked to a certain extent.

The work of the Administration in this branch of the service, it seems to us, cannot be commended too highly. Business men have offered their services freely and willingly to aid the production end of aviation in the most efficient manner. Many aeroplanes are being turned out, and training schools, fully equipped, have sprung up in six weeks' time. Judging from this school, the class of boys who are enlisting in this branch of the service is fine. I feel confident that the aviation service will quickly respond to the war's demands.

I am so much interested in the work here that I would do nothing to delay my commission, or retard getting to the front for active service, but must confess that I rather envy father at present. He is at his wonderful salmon river in northern Canada. Another record fishing season seems to have given him the vigour of youth. He wrote me that he had a fine visit with Mr. and Mrs. Braithwaite in Montreal and I am sure that he and my sisters will join me in remembrance to you.

Your affectionate cousin,

William M. Russel.

To Miss Anne M. Hendrie,
Bank of Montreal,
Threadneedle Street,
London, England.

Fourth Aerial Squadron,
Rantoul, Illinois,
July 20, 1917.

Dear Father—

The hard times seem to have passed, and things have quickly rounded into shape. On the fourth day, our blankets, mattresses and beds arrived, and on the following day, even greater luxuries came. We were ordered to report at the Quartermaster's without notice for what purpose, and there, to our surprise, received sheets and pillows. A very essential thing, however, namely, food, is not yet conveniently provided. The announcement that the mess hall would open last Monday was welcomed with great acclaim, but it would have been better if the doors of the temple had remained closed.

The service is so new that it does not meet the demand, and lead poisoning arising from the new plumbing has spoiled the water and interfered with the cooking. Ten of the boys are laid up in the hospital at Champaign, three of them quite sick.

Flying is progressing better than at either of our former fields. Monday, we resumed systematic flying, and the weather has been ideal until today, when it was very rough. I have been able to get my thirty minutes each day, and really begin to feel like a regular aviator, even if I do place a lot of faith in that young man in the front seat who can set me right if I go wrong. It seems, sometimes, as though I would be lost without him. They tell me that you never get real confidence until you have made some solo flights.

Today was a Jonah for us. In the afternoon, ten of the more advanced students tried their Reserve Military Aviator tests, with some disappointing results. Nervous, but determined, they all started off brilliantly. The first test was to climb to an altitude of four thousand feet, and remain there forty-five minutes, then descend into the field and land within one hundred and fifty feet of a designated stake.

The first, in descending, misjudged his distance, rolled by the pylon, and bumped into another machine. The captain was wrought up, and he had hardly turned away from the wreck when the second machine crashed head-on into a pile of lumber. The boy's head was thrown forward, hitting the cowl, and he was badly bruised about the face. A remarkable incident of the accident was that he did not have time to remove his goggles, and when his head was thrown forward, they struck the celluloid wind shield, and were broken.

Just before going up, he borrowed a pair of triplex glasses from one of the other boys. The glass in the goggles was cracked into a million sections, and not a particle splintered. This triplex glass is a safety device either of mica compound or glass between thin strips of mica. If you can find a pair in Detroit, Boston, or New York, please buy them for me. They are quite expensive, and, I understand, nearly all in this country have been sold. Get a large field of vision—the small ones are not useful. I am enclosing a sketch of the best size and shape.

Now for more trouble. Not fifteen minutes later, two machines came down, and nosed over, breaking the propellers. This is caused by the wheels sticking in the mud or a rut, which throws the tail up and tips the propeller into the ground. Usually nothing more serious happens than to put the machine out of commission for a while.

Yesterday, our corps was increased by the transfer of eighteen very fine fellows from the winter school at Miami, Florida.

An order came today, directing ten of the young men here to report in New York within twenty-four hours, to sail for France. They seem to have picked the men at random, and we cannot understand how it was done. It has caused great discussion, and we cannot surmise who will be called next. It was not the especially good flyers, mechanics or leaders who were chosen.

The two French officers who have been stationed here are both fine and interesting fellows. They think that our machines, the Curtis, J. N. 4 B., are the best training machines they have seen, and say that when we go to Europe we will have to learn how to fly four different types of machines, including the monoplanes. They have not yet become accustomed to flying our machines, and they have given very little exhibition flying. I spoke to Maury about Colonel Littebrant's kind suggestion of positions in his regiment. It might be a great opportunity for some of the boys, but we feel very well satisfied with our chance to become aviators. Maury's mother used to be a dear friend of Mrs. Littebrant's in St. Louis, and Maury thought his brother Walker might be interested. If he is, I will let you know by telegram within a couple of days.

We have been ordered to wear uniforms all the time now, so I will send my civilian clothes home. Maury has gone home for a visit.

Even if I could get away, I feel that I could not leave without hindering my instruction and progress, but longing to see you, I am,

Your loving son,

William.

Fourth Aerial Squadron,
Rantoul, Illinois,
July 23, 1917.

Dear Christine—

No wonder you could not locate me. We are very much buried in this little town in Illinois.

It was rumoured, but not definitely known, that we were leaving Ashburn, until just before an order came to set the machines in perfect condition to be prepared to fly to Rantoul at five o'clock next morning. Everyone wanted to take an aeroplane, or go as a pilot, but hopes were shattered when word came that only instructors and advanced students should fly, and that each should be accompanied by a mechanic. It would have been quite an experience, as well as good training, to fly cross-country for one hundred and fourteen miles.

It was a wonderful sight to watch the twenty-five machines, in the early morning, circle out of the field, one closely following the other, to an altitude of three thousand feet, and then strike south. They averaged about eighty miles an hour, and dropped into the field at Rantoul in the same order. One machine only, driven by Mr. Pond, my new instructor, was forced to land in the town of Kankakee for gasoline. In starting his motor again, the mechanic did not get out of the way of the propeller quickly enough, and was slightly hurt. Aside from this small accident, the trip was made with a clean record. The trip, for the rest of us, however, was not so pleasant. We left Ashburn about 10:30 in the morning, and wandered over the tracks at a slow pace, covering the hundred miles by 10:30 in the evening, with practically nothing to eat all day.

In a hot, stuffy coach, you can imagine how happy and congenial the crowd was when at last we ran into Rantoul. Even the reception which awaited us—the entire town assembled in Sunday clothes, ginghams and overalls, with a band of music, waving flags, and a kind greeting from everyone, old and young—did not cheer us into amiability. We were immediately ordered to march to the field and the new barracks. After a long walk through the mud, we were halted before a low, white building, which, in the night, looked like a bowling alley, and told that these were our future quarters. A rush for bed followed, but to our dismay, there were only thirty beds and a few blankets for eighty tired men. Morning was welcome, and everyone was up at early daybreak for a change. Getting up was a rest for aching bones.

No breakfast could be served because the mess hall was not finished, and we were told to subsist on the country. This was difficult, because there was then nothing like a restaurant in the little town, and the farmers being all well-to-do, as they said, did not have to take boarders. It was nearly four days before cots, blankets and convenient food were to be had. Since then, life has been bearable, but the comforts of home seem like a dream.

But the purpose of coming here, namely, flying, has been well met. The weather has been ideal, and great progress has been made. I have had a thirty-minute flight every day. The training has been slow on account of frequent removals, but at last I am getting to the end of my preliminary instruction. For the past few days I have been working on landings, which is the final step. Next, solo work, or flying alone, begins in preparation for the Reserve Military Aviator tests. If these are passed, my commission follows automatically.

The work becomes more fascinating each day, and as instruction continues, you realise that flying is a science with something more always to learn. A person can easily learn enough in one week to fly in the air, but without more experience, he would lose his confidence and have an accident at a critical moment. This has been evident during the last few days. Many of the boys became impatient, and induced their instructors to turn them loose for solo work.

Friday, we had four accidents, none of them serious, but the machines were wrecked and the boys pretty well bruised up—all due to ignorance and inexperience in the pinches. Then Saturday, one of my room-mates in Chicago was sure he could make a good landing. The controls were turned over to him by the instructor, and when he came down he was sailing against the wind at an air speed of about seventy miles an hour—that is, going at the rate of fifty miles against a wind of twenty.

In flying, you calculate your speed with the air and not the ground, as it is the pressure against the wings which does the lifting. So when he rounded the last turn to alight in the field, the twenty miles wind pressure was taken away, because he was then flying with the wind, and not against it, and the air speed was reduced to not more than forty miles an hour, which is below the necessary minimum. The machine went into a tail spin at an altitude of about 200 feet, and crashed to the ground. Both occupants were taken from the plane and given up for dead. On examination, however, to our great joy, they were found to be badly cut and their noses broken and faces disfigured, but luckily without permanent serious injuries, although the machine was a total wreck.

I wish I could explain some of the ways of getting into a tail spin, but am too young in the art yet, and it is difficult for me to describe it. Even with a perfect machine, it is only one of many dangerous situations which may come at any minute. A flyer must know how to avoid them if possible, and to counteract them if necessary.

A fine letter from father came, which gave me mingled joy and grief. His description of life on the Petit Pabos brought the camp and river here. I could see the salmon and hear the waters. It sounds too good to be true. He has had another great year, with a new record catch in numbers and size. I have delightful plans in mind, but can only hope they will be realised. If I become a successful solo flyer, I will ask for ten days' leave and visit father on Cape Cod. I am also thinking of asking for a transfer to the Aerial Squadron at Detroit— that is, Mt. Clemens. It is possible, being an advanced student, that at a new school, I may get a better commission. These are the castles in the air which I am building. The only work done so far has been to talk over the plans and specifications with Captain Spain.

Your meeting the twelve aeronauts sent over by the French Government is rather a coincidence. Two of them, Lieutenants Prevot and Laffiy, are stationed here, and I have become very well acquainted with them. They are interesting men, as you say, and good fellows as well.

The Loon Lake pictures which you sent make me envious. This is a better flying country, however, and not being summer visitors, suits our purposes better than your attractive scenery.

Love to Allen and all the kids.

                    Your affectionate brother,

                                        William.

To Mrs. Allen F. Edwards,
Detroit, Mich.

                              Fourth Aerial Squadron,
                                   Rantoul, Illinois,
                                   July 26, 1917.

Dear Father—

Again, we have had hard luck. Another serious accident happened Saturday, but the two occupants escaped miraculously well. Evans Baxter, my former room-mate at Chicago, and his instructor were the unfortunates. It was a case of the same old tail spin too near the ground. They were dropping down into the field from a high altitude on a long glide, and lost too much headway. About two hundred and fifty feet from the ground, the wind caught the tail of the machine and spun it around. Both kept their heads remarkably well, and if they had had fifteen feet more in which to drop, they would have avoided the smash. They straightened out just enough to break the fall, and when they collided with the ground, their life belts held their bodies firm, but their heads were thrown forward against the cowl. Both faces cut and disfigured and one nose broken was the score. Then the day following, the worst of our accidents happened, and it was on the ground. Our little mail boy, riding his motorcycle down for the mail, was struck by an automobile at a side street. His leg was so badly crushed that they were unable to get any impulse, and it was necessary to amputate below the knee. These accidents have been the main topic of our conversation, and so they are the first things in my mind as I write you.

Everything has not been unpleasant, however. We have had much to brighten us. In the first place, our mess has been improved, and under the last war act, our pay as flying sergeants has been increased from forty-four dollars to one hundred dollars a month, beginning August 1st, and our allowance for rations, from thirty-five cents to seventy-five cents a day. We were the last of the Reserve Army to receive this increased pay. It seems peculiar that the Aviation Corps is the last, when all of us who pass the tests are sure to receive commissions.

In the other branches, commissions may or may not follow. More good news was the coming of ten new Curtis planes yesterday. This will give us a chance for more instruction, which, however, is progressing rapidly now. I have reached the step where I am making landings. This is a difficult part of flying, and to a considerable extent, the phase by which you are judged. It is no easy thing for me yet, but I am sure I will soon get the knack of it. My instructor said yesterday that my air work was tip-top, and that I was coming on with the landings. Tuesday and Wednesday, I practiced gliding into the field from an altitude of two thousand feet. That was easy, but when we got about one hundred and fifty feet from the ground, he would take the control and make the landings. I would then ascend, and we would do the same thing over and over again. The purpose of this is to practice your spirals so that you will enter the field from the right side and always against the wind.

I ran out of funds quite suddenly the other day—not from any loss, however. It was before the mess had improved, and I was buying and paying for each meal. I have not had time to write, because there has been so much work on the machines for inspection.

I have at last had an aeroplane put under my supervision, for which I am wholly responsible, and which is also my own instruction machine. This puts an incentive up to you for careful work, as your neck depends upon your own diligence.

A package has just come from Aunt Jennie and Aunt Chris, containing knitted helmets, which I am told will be very necessary when the weather becomes colder. I have never worn a knitted one yet, and it does not seem at present that I would ever want one. The weather is roasting, and we have to work all day in the broiling sun with heavy flannels and woollen shirts, the only wear for soldiers. We have to be in uniform always now.

I had a fine letter from Christine a couple of days ago, telling all about her cottage at Loon Lake, and enclosing pictures of the beautiful country. It is certainly more attractive than Rantoul, but I could not see that there were any streams there, and if I cannot get fishing, I will take flying, and I think now that I am beginning to prefer soaring to wading.

Your loving son,

William.

Fourth Aerial Squadron,
Rantoul, Illinois,
August 1, 1917.

Dear Father—
The last few days have been exceptionally busy and terribly hot.

My flight today is last on the list, and my machine is running like a bird, so that I have a few minutes for a breathing spell and retreat from the burning sun. Monday morning, when I began instruction, we had a very poor machine, and the air was rough. I have told you accidents usually occur if you lose headway near the ground, either on the first turn in ascending, or the last turn in descending. The predicament we were in Monday was a perfect setting for such trouble. In climbing from the field with a motor which was not working too well, we could not get enough altitude, and had to take the first turn when only seventy-five feet in the air.

Mr. Pond, my instructor, was watchful, as he always is, and grasped the situation and took the controls from me, and dropped into the field with the wind, something that is never done except in emergencies. We landed all right, but he refused to go up again until the machine was fixed. I worked on it for more than two hours—changed the propeller and some other minor things—and then called Mr. Pond. He then tried it alone, but found it unsatisfactory, and condemned it. This put me to work for the day. It meant that the entire motor had to be removed from the fuselage, and another set in. Allen Wardle and I tackled the job, and we have since been working and sweating steadily—Monday night until eight o'clock, and last night until nine. This morning, we tried her out, and found her satisfactory. She will turn over thirteen hundred and twenty-five revolutions a minute—twenty-five more than the mark. This, of course, is on the ground. In the air, she will turn over about one hundred better.

Mr. Pond is a very conservative instructor. He has a method of teaching which is different from the others, and I am becoming convinced that he is right, although at first, I envied some of the other boys their more daring teachers. The common way of instructing is to give four or five lessons in air work, right and left turns, and straight flying; then start immediately upon landings, and having accomplished this, turn you loose. In this course, you seem to be making very rapid progress. Mr. Pond, on the other hand, gives you twenty-five or thirty lessons in air work. He claims that landings then come naturally to you.

You are judged in your progress, however, by the other students, according to the number of lessons you have had in landings, and when you say you have had none, they think you are not getting ahead. I felt this way until I had a long talk with Mr. Pond, and have reasoned out the matter. Up to now, I have had twenty-two lessons in the air on right and left turns, and in gliding. He says that my work has been good, and that he would start me on landings this morning. If I catch on all right, I have great hopes of doing solo work by the end of next week if we have good weather. I am looking forward to it with delight.

Bob Townes drove me over to Chicago for Sunday in his auto. Regular beds, hotel meals, and above all, a hot bath, which as yet is a luxury in Rantoul, made the trip worthwhile. In the evening, we went to the South Shore Country Club, and had a regular swim in Lake Michigan; just think of it! Sunday, also, I had a happy time with Bill Davidson. He is in the artillery at Fort Sheridan.

While we were away, another dreadful accident happened, which put a deep gloom over the post. A fine young fellow, named Mitchell, assigned to the Tenth Squadron, also stationed here, tried to jump a freight to ride over to Champaign. His foot slipped, and he went under the moving train and was instantly killed. There was a military funeral yesterday. The squadron marched to the train with the body, which was sent to Texas, the boy's home.

The little mail boy, now one-legged, is getting along well.

Here we are, at an aviation school, and the only two accidents resulting in the loss of life or limb thus far have been automobile and railroad casualties.

The first seven students turned out from this school have been placed on the instructing staff. They were given their commissions, and each has a class. Whether a similar fate shall fall to our lot, I do not know. While this flying game is most attractive to me, I have never wanted to be an instructor. The plan seems to be to split the students here into bunches—some are assigned to instruction—some to Fort Wood, from whence, we understand, they will be sent directly to France for further instruction. It is possible, after such advanced course, that they will be recalled to instruct in this country. In enlisting now, we learn that they wish to know whether one wants to go into the army or in the Lafayette Esquadrille. In the latter, I think a boy will get immediate service.

I feel sure that it will be impossible for me to visit you at Osterville. It is not easy to get a leave, and at the present stage, I do not want to miss an hour's practice. I will see you surely, however, in September in Detroit.

What have you thought about my trying to get a transfer to Mt. Clemens so as to be near home? In a week, my instruction will be finished, and then it simply means that I spend so much time in the air until I can take the R. M. A. tests, when I will be assigned to service for which I am anxiously waiting.

Advise me about the transfer. Give my love to all.

Your loving son,

William.

Fourth Aerial Squadron,
Rantoul, Illinois,
August 5, 1917.

Dear Father—

The heat for the last few days has simply burned up this flat, dry country. It has been necessary for me to remain in the field under the broiling sun practically all day long in order to keep the record of the flights, and to see that the machines are filled with gasoline and in running order. This gave me headaches at first, and just as I was beginning to become accustomed to it, we adopted a new plan. We asked Mr. Pond if he would not instruct the men on landings early in the morning so we could have the benefit of the cool, still air. After some discussion, he assented, so now, Bill Goulding, Allen Wardle and I drive down in Bill's car and pick him up for breakfast and return to the field for flying at 5:30 in the morning. With this early start, we are able to finish before the hot noon sun, and have more time to work on the machines in the shade before the flights begin at 1:30 for the solo men.

I have come to the conclusion that making a landing is the trick of flying. Last week, I would willingly have taken up a machine alone, with the expectation of having a pleasant trip and an easy finish, but this week, I would not touch one. My first lessons in landing, I am frank to say, scared me considerably. My instructions were to sit back with my hands off the control and watch every move. Next, I was to handle the controls myself. I rose from the ground, circled the field, and endeavoured to drop in from the same side from which I left, so as to be continually against the wind.

The sensation of having the ground rushing by you, as well as rapidly approaching you, tends to make you somewhat dizzy at first. I brought her down within about fifty feet of the ground, and then gave up. Mr. Pond landed her that time. Then I made another attempt. This time, it was not a good landing, but I felt a little more at ease. It becomes more and more natural, and at last a mere incident of the flying. The trick lies in attempting to judge your altitude and the length of the glide in order to land at a certain spot. I am catching on and if good weather continues, have great hopes of soloing by the end of next week. It remains for me to judge my distances better and perfect the touch on the earth. My landings, as yet, are rather erratic.

Yesterday afternoon, we had a leave, and started for Champaign, but, by the time we had walked to the interurban station, we were so hot that we gave up the trip, and went to the Rantoul cafeteria and had a refrigerator lunch. The menu was luxurious for us—iced tea, cold sliced peaches and ice cream ad lib. M. E. Carter then took us to his house—the Carters have taken one in Rantoul—and we played bridge all the afternoon with a flagon of ice cold lemonade kept full to the brim within reach. Thus, we managed to survive the heat.

Today, Maury and I got up early and had breakfast in the restaurant, and read the morning papers, where the big electric fan cools the air.

The news from Russia looks bad once more, with the resignation of Kerensky. We had begun to pin our faith and hope on him.

You don't say anything about my transfer to Detroit. I would like to leave Rantoul and its warmth if possible, but have not said anything to Major Dunworth, as I felt that you might not approve the change.

Although we were fortunate here in being exempt, last week seemed to be another period of accidents. At Mineola, a student and an instructor were killed; at Bay Shore, two were killed; and in West Virginia, a student was killed. It is peculiar the way these accidents come in groups. The nearest we came to trouble was that two machines, through carelessness, rose from the ground about the same time, and nearly collided. We have had warning and strict injunction to avoid this, and I think it is not likely to happen again here.

There was an order given out today that no one can have a pass to leave for more than twenty-four hours, so I am afraid that this will surely cut out my chances to visit Osterville.

Hoping you are as well as I am, but cooler, I remain,

   Your loving son,

              William.

           Fourth Aerial Squadron,
             Rantoul, Illinois,
             August 11, 1917.

Dear Father—

At last I am a regular aviator. I realised it with surprise and some nervousness.

Wednesday, I was placed in the back seat and told to continue my instruction in making landings. Every one I made was poor. The slump stayed with me until Friday. I "pan-caked" as they call it, every time. At a height of about two hundred feet, you throttle down your motor. This tips the front part of the machine down, and causes you to glide. Once in a gliding position, it is necessary to hold the front end up, or she will dive too rapidly. You continue your glide earthward until you get within about thirty feet of the ground, when you steepen your glide in order to obtain more speed. This is the difficult part of landing, because you become nervous, and the natural tendency is to level off too high from the ground. The steep glide should be held until you are very close to the ground—then you level out and hold her in the air as long as possible until she settles to the earth.

In the few days, while I was in my slump, on getting near to the ground, I would get nervous and level off about ten feet from the earth, and then, when I lost speed, I would drop to the ground with a bump. Friday, I broke the wing-skid and blew the right tire in a careless landing, I pancaked, and was lifted back into the air from the heavy bump. The wind got under my left wing, and threw me over on my right side, and broke the tire and skid. It was not very serious, but caused half an hour's delay, and deprived me of that much practice. Yesterday, however, I was determined to make good. I headed the list, and got the benefit of the still early morning air. My first landing was poor, and my instructor had to help me with it. The next three, however, were beauties. I did them all alone, and set the machine on the ground like a basket of eggs.

Without another word said, Mr. Pond stepped out of the front seat, lifted the tail around so as to point the nose of the machine to the wind, and said, "Go ahead, Russel, let's see you take her up alone." Never before had I missed company so much, but my chance had come at last, so I gave her all the throttle, and started. Taking her off the ground was simple enough, and the air work was even more so, and I felt no worry except for the lack of companionship.

At first, it seemed awful to be alone in the wide, wide sky. I thought of the *Ancient Mariner,* which I used to hate so in the Detroit University School because I had to study it: "So lonesome 'twas that God Himself scarce seemed there to be." When I approached the spot where I had to start my glide for the ground, the nervousness returned. Before, when I was in this situation, I would merely throw up my hands, and Mr. Pond would bring her down; but here I was, about

121

three hundred feet high, and no way to bring her down except to do it myself. My involuntary prayer was, "Why did you let Mr. Pond lie to me. Oh Lord, and tell me I could do it?"

I reached the point I thought was right, cut off the motor, clinched my hands on the wheel, and started for the ground at about fifty miles an hour. The next thing I remember, I was rolling along the ground, and had made the best landing possible. Mr. Pond came up and said, "Very good. Try it again." This time it was more simple, and there was less nervousness in the atmosphere, and I finished with equal success; then I tried it two or three times more, and found that I was getting some confidence in myself. A little more experience, and less self-doubt (it seems that I never thought enough of myself), and I will be all right. After the first solo flight, I felt as if I had some right to wear an aviator's uniform.

Friday night was an interesting evening in camp. The instruction in night flying began. The more advanced students, under the pupilage of Lieutenants Laffly, Prevot, and Captain Brown, made the flights. It was a weird and astonishing exhibition, and surely tries the nerves. On one of the hangars five strong searchlights were placed; four gleaming out into the field, and one directly into the zenith. The aeroplane was brought out into the light, started, and was out of sight in a second. Then we could only hear the roar of the motor. Away from the shafts of light you could not see the machine, even close to the ground. We could hear it circle about the field a couple of times, and then it passed through the light like a flash and disappeared.

The next minute, the motor had been cut down, and everybody waited breathlessly for the landing. In a second, the machine passed into the light, coming at a tremendous speed. Some three hundred feet beyond it touched the ground with a beautiful tail-high landing, a thing which is usually discouraged. Lieutenant Laffly told me after-wards that he dropped fifteen hundred feet in a short distance into the field, and this accounted for his terrific speed. It is hard to explain it to you, but it was really the most thrilling flight I have ever watched. Probably it was so interesting to me because the task of landing in the day time is still so difficult for me. There were two other flights that evening.

Friday, we had inspection before General George O. Squier and other notable gentlemen, including our fellow townsmen, Howard Coffin, Roy Chapin and Goodloe Edgar. They were not associating with sergeants, and none of them recognised me. Several of them had rides in the air. As I did not talk with Coffin or Chapin, I did not get the information from them, but there is a rumour that the Hudson factory will soon be devoted entirely to the manufacture of aeroplane motors.

Maury Hill had a nasty accident yesterday. He was cranking one of the machines, which, as you know, are started by the propeller, and it back-fired, and nearly broke his wrist. It gave him a bad three-inch cut on the wrist. This morning it is very stiff, but he can move his fingers, so for a wonder, it does not seem to be broken. To be sure, he is going to Champaign to have an X-ray taken this afternoon.

Today, Sunday, the day of rest, we have the pleasant task of setting up ten new machines which came last night from the Curtis factory. Orders are that we shall continue work until all are set up ready for flight tomorrow morning. It won't be part of the day's work—it will be all of it. The last letter to me, with the desired enclosure, was lost for a week. Somebody laid it on my cot, and when I was making my bed in the morning, I folded it in and put it to sleep. I got it on the 9th, and the post mark was the 31st. We have received no pay yet.

On account of several of the boys' carelessness in failing to return on time, leaves have been limited to forty-eight hours, and only one a month, so it is a sure thing I will not be able to go to Osterville. I will try to visit you in Detroit on your return.

Hoping you are all well and happy, I remain

Your loving son,

William.

Fourth Aerial Squadron,
Rantoul, Illinois,
August 17, 1917.

Dear Father—

All efforts to get a leave seem to be in vain. One thing or another comes up which prevents a leave for even forty-eight hours. After I began soloing, I thought I would get a couple of weeks' furlough, but now I am disappointed in this. Lieutenant Hines, in charge of solo flying, was wrought up last Sunday because there were only two men to help him bring the machines out in the field, so he refused to sign any more passes, and Lieutenant Fleckenger will not sign any which exempt men from class work. My only hope is for a leave in September for a visit to Detroit.

Work now is about the same as before, with a little change in the hours. At present I report at 4:30 a. m., and work through until twelve o'clock. The next day I begin at twelve o'clock noon, and work through until the machine is ready for the next day's flying. I have to keep a record of each man's flight, and to see that the machines are in good running condition while I am on duty. Of course, I have time out for my flight, one-half hour each day, and for my classes. The end of the week will, no doubt, bring the last stage of my training (elementary), and then I will take the tests to qualify as a Reserve Military Aviator. There are six tests to be met:

(1) To climb to an altitude of four thousand feet and remain there half an hour.

(2) To make a cross-country flight of sixty miles without a stop.

(3) Cross-country flight to the town of Leroy (forty miles) with a stop there.

(4) To jump an obstacle fifteen feet high, and come to a stop within fifteen hundred feet of the obstacle.

(5) To climb out of a field two thousand feet square to an altitude of five hundred feet. (This is really the most difficult and dangerous.)

(6) To cut off your motor at an altitude of a thousand feet, and glide to the earth, landing within two hundred feet of a fixed mark.

The last requires much skill and practice. Having passed these tests, my first training will be over, and I am recommended for a commission. I would like then to be transferred to Mt. Clemens, because there one is assigned to active duty again. On completion of these tests, the future work is problematical. It may be instructing, or being instructed in the use of the machine gun, bombing and other military aeronautic tactics.

Last week, Mr. Goodloe Edgar found me out. I was at my usual work when an orderly informed me I was wanted at headquarters. Captain Edgar was waiting for me there, and was very courteous. He told me that the school at Selfridge (Mt. Clemens) was to be an advanced school, and hinted that it would be a good place for me to go. Another thing he said which you will be interested in learning, was that a great number of us would not be sent overseas at all, but would be kept in this country as instructors. When the time for the transfer comes, I will let you know. You may be able to accomplish things with all that Detroit contingent.

Another thing I would like to have you do, if you think it is right, is to get my commission issued as soon as possible after it has been recommended. You may be able to get things done quickly at Washington, as you did before. Without somebody to push it, my commission may stagnate in Washington, or be lost, the same as my first application for enlistment from Cornell. You remember that we could not find it, and had to put in a new application at Washington. This thing of spurring them on at Washington, which I am asking, is not unusual. Several of the Memphis boys have had their Senator and other influential people do it for them.

You speak of my discomfort. You can forget it. It is not as bad as I may have painted it. We are probably as comfortable here as we deserve. The students are now separate from the regulars, both in barracks and meals. We have new quarters up in the officers' end of the post. The mess is much better. We have given enough of our pay to the mess sergeant to enable him to hire cooks, but we have no waiters yet, and we still serve, wash up the dishes and pans, and are the kitchen police. You may laugh, but washing dishes is the most disagreeable, dirty work I ever had to do. It turns my stomach to wash plates covered with the thick, sticky food served here. In fact, my stomach has been slow to adopt the army diet. I am very well, but often go without meals, and at times, have obtained a pass to eat down town. It is a great inconvenience, but seems to be the saving clause for me. I think, however, I will soon be able to eat and wash anything with anybody.

I was fortunate the other day in being able to pick up a fine pair of triplex goggles in Chicago. Also, you will be interested in knowing I have a wrist watch. The day I began soloing, I found that my prejudice against it was sentimental, and on the next day I hastened to get one. In the air you want to know the time, and you cannot fumble around in your pockets to find a watch. You are only allowed half an hour for your flying, and the order is strict not to over-run your time. In feeling around for my watch, I nearly had an unexpected loop. So now, the wrist watch for me, and no remarks.

I remember Dwight Armstrong very well. Give him my regards. I have not seen him since leaving Hill.

No chance of Osterville for me this year. In place of that we will have our visit and golf or a long ride together in Detroit.

With love to all,

Your loving son,

William.

125

Dear Father—

The interval between my letters has been longer than usual, but not because I have not been thinking of you all. I have had my first touch of discouragement this past week.

Our commanding officers have all been changed, and four majors of the regular army are in charge. They seem to think that greater discipline for the reserves is necessary, and they are certainly putting them through their paces. We have about two hundred regulars here who do not fly, and have been doing the fatigue detail, but now they do nothing, and the reserves are required to do all the work, even waiting on the tables, and serving the regulars, and washing their dishes, and cleaning up their garbage.

Next, we have not been permitted to take our R. M. A. tests, which were set for last Tuesday. An announcement is made that we must have fifteen hours of solo work instead of four, which has been considered ample for any normal person. This means possibly another six weeks' training before tests, and is delaying our entire course. This is on the safety-first side, of course, and maybe it ought not to be objected to, but another thing which goes against the grain and is contrary to the promise made on our enlistment, is that administrators and men in charge of fields only are to be recommended for commissions, the others to be flying sergeants. The former are all regulars, and exposed to no danger. The sergeants would do the fighting.

Young regulars, too, most of whom enlisted after we did, have been placed in charge of sections of about ten reserves. These men, who have had little or no experience, and do not fly, and are surely not as well qualified as the class of men in the aviation reserves, have the say as to whether a machine is in condition to fly. This change has come within a week, and naturally a gloom has come with it. Our consolation is that we are confident that such regulations must be only temporary.

My own flying has advanced satisfactorily, and I am beginning at last to believe more in myself. On Friday and Monday, conditions for flying were very bad, and after a few flights, flying was called off, I went up both days, and cruised about with a forty-mile wind blowing. By exercising watchful care, the rise, the flight in the air, and the landing were all satisfactory. I was rather surprised that there was not more bother, and this experience, more than anything else so far, has given me confidence. They were not the usual pleasant flights, as there was a fight every minute to keep stable, first a bump on one side, then on the other, then a drop, and in a fraction of a second you would go shooting directly up. All the time you had to watch yourself; going with the wind, the speed would be about one hundred miles an hour, and against it, not much more than twenty. It seems to me that I learned more in those two half-hour storm flights than in all the rest of my time. A minute's practice in the exercise of quick judgment and the correction of errors caused by nasty weather counts more than hours of smooth sailing.

Maury invited me to visit him in St. Louis over Sunday. I had no money, but, of course, I went. Speaking of money, you may be wondering what I do with the lavish wages which I receive. The fact is, we have not received any for July or August. On the sergeant's door is the following notice:

Please do not bother me with foolish and unimportant questions as to when you will get your pay.

At St. Louis we spent Sunday evening at Sunset Inn, where my St. Louis college friends gathered. Nearly everyone was in uniform, and had been since about July 1st. Sunday, we had a fine day at the Country Club, and I played golf like an aviator. We travelled all night, and were back in the field bright and early, and in time for work Monday morning.

I would like to go to Detroit a week from next Saturday. Can you not arrange my matters there so that it will require about five days to attend to them?

There is much talk about where we will go for the winter. It may be Memphis again, or Waco, Texas, or possibly stay here. From the progress already made, I think that I might save time and get into action quicker by going to Mt. Clemens. That is something I would like to look over in Detroit.

A nice letter and a bunch of magazines came from Christine the other day. Several of the articles in the Atlantic were very interesting, and have brought about some useful discussion among the boys. If this series of articles continues, please keep the magazine coming.

We are busier than ever, and we now have the new duty of two hours' military drill each day. I also regret to say that it is necessary to repeat my vaccination and inoculations again. It seems that the doctor failed to make record in his register in my case and several others. It is a bit of a calamity, and I think that Dr. Brown was, too. We like our new physician very much.

This is far from a cheerful letter, but here's hoping that the next will be bright and full of sunshine, which is here aplenty. We think that the worst is *not* yet to come.

I am enclosing a small photo which Bill Goulding snapped of me with my fighting face on, just before my first solo. You will observe a few signs of nervousness. Otherwise it is a very good picture, as he now appears, of

Your loving son,

William.

Chanute Field,
Rantoul, Illinois,
September 3, 1917.

Dear Anne—

This is the first of my letters to Detroit addressed to you, but I knew that of course you would see my letters to father. Today, I felt like having a talk with you from far away.

My work has been fascinating with only occasional draw backs. Until we came to Rantoul, little was accomplished, but since then, progress has been so fast that I can hardly realise all my preliminary training is over, and now it is only to wait until my commission arrives and I am assigned to active duty. Today, the last of my R. M. A. tests was successfully completed. This makes me a Reserve Military Aviator. The final tests are extended during three days. First, we were required to climb to an altitude of four thousand feet and remain there forty-five minutes. On the descent, we had to make one spiral to the right and one to the left with the motor shut down. The drop into the field was made with a dead engine from a height of one thousand feet, and the landing within two hundred feet of a designated mark. This is not the most dangerous, but by far the hardest to do accurately.

The next was a triangular cross-country flight, covering a distance of sixty miles without a stop. Then, there were three tests, consisting of climbing to an altitude of five hundred feet without going out of the boundaries of a tract two thousand feet square. This is the most dangerous, because one is apt to get into a tail spin on the turns, which is very perilous if you are near the ground. Next, on landing, we had to jump a hurdle fifteen feet high, and land on the other side, coming to a stop within fifteen hundred feet of the hurdle; and last of all, a

CHANUTE FIELD, RANTOUL, ILL.
FIRST SOLO FLIGHT, AUGUST 11, 1917

hundred-mile cross-country flight without a stop. I am informed now that I am entitled to a commission, but it may be some time before it comes. It seems to take longer in the aviation than in the other branches of the service.

Our life here, during the time when we do not have the excitement and delight of flying, is very monotonous, and under strict regulations. The bugler blows his horn so often, from early morning until evening, and each time we must jump up and answer, "Here." What little time one might have for recreation, is carefully occupied for recitations, lectures, or some fatigue duty. Such things as washing dishes, unloading coal from cars, policing the quarters and building roads are common forms of fatigue duty; and the worst is, if you are unfortunate enough to draw one of these fatigues during the time set apart for your flight, you have to give up flying. Nevertheless, we are training to be aviators. We are persuaded, too, that the three majors in charge have no affection for reserves, but we must give them credit for pushing us along. At other training camps, I understand Saturdays and Sundays are free, and furloughs are frequently granted, but our Sunday is not a day of rest, and furloughs, except upon good cause shown, are nil.

Our quarters are very comfortable, but there is no chance to be alone. You eat, wash, dress, sleep, and even write with a throng about you. You might not like the food, but it is wholesome and nutritious. One thing we seriously object to is the fondness which our medical staff have for vaccinating and inoculating. I have been scraped for small pox twice, and injected for typhoid three times. I am told the small pox game is now concluded, but the doctor says that several more typhoid preventatives may be sufficient.

My thoughts in idle moments now all turn to home, and I am endeavouring to concoct a plan which will commend itself to Major Brown for a visit to Detroit. I have been nearly five months away, and have missed only one-half a day of work, when I spent Sunday at home. If I can get away now, among other enjoyments of home will be an appointment with the dentist.

Well, Anne, after leaving college, here I am, in an army post, taking a post graduate course, learning to fly and fight. What will happen when my commission comes, or even before, I do not know. All kinds of rumours are afloat. Some of the boys have been sent to other schools in America as instructors, and others to England, France, Italy and Egypt for further instruction in aeronautical war tactics.

Hoping to see you all soon.

Your loving brother.

Bill.

To Mrs. James T. McMillan,
Grosse Pointe Park, Mich.

Fourth Aerial Squadron,
Rantoul, Illinois,
September 11, 1917.

Dear Father—

The R. M. A. tests, as I wrote you, are completed. I am considered a finished aviator as far as the instruction at this camp goes, and am now only waiting for a commission and the assignment to active duty. Those of us who have passed, have little to do but wait. The others have preference in the use of the machines, and only when one is idle do we get a ride. I have managed, however, by being ready at any minute, to squeeze in a fifteen or twenty-minute flight each day. There is a pleasing rumour today that the boys who have passed may be sent home to await their commissions and assignments to active duty, although I have been turned down for a leave, and feel sure that my expected visit home must be given up. It seems that we must not be scattered, and must be on call for assignment on short notice.

Last night, the class which preceded us was sent, on telegraphic order, to San Antonio, Texas, for advanced training. Orders were given at reveille, and twenty-four of the boys were off the next morning. Many of them were my friends at Memphis, and I felt rotten when they said goodbye. Several pairs of brothers and many best friends were split up. To those of us who were left, not even a reliable hint, except that we may expect a removal soon, has been given as to where we will go, whether to Memphis, Miami, San Antonio, France, Italy or Egypt.

I have not bought any officer's uniform yet, because we are told that probably a new style will be worn by the Aviation Section, steel grey in colour, with a soft roll collar. It will be an innovation, and until we know definitely, you will see no change in my comfortable undress soldier clothes. The weather now has become very cold, and we are having our first taste of winter flying. I do not dread it, because I am sure the excitement of flying will keep your mind off the weather, and keep you warm all right.

If you should run across Captain Edgar, or Major Hutton, give them my regards, and please let them know that I have completed my instruction and am waiting for a commission.

I am very well, a little too fit if anything, and have nothing to complain of except that I cannot visit you.

Love to all,

Your loving son,

William.

Telegram

Champaign, Illinois,
September 11, 1917.

Henry Russel,
Detroit.

Word received from Washington this evening, ordering us to report immediately to Camp Kelly, San Antonio, for advanced training on speed scout machines. Will wire you further information and address, Maury and I are separated. Very sorry for that. Ten of us to leave.

William.

Telegram

Rantoul, Illinois,
September 12, 1917.

Henry Russel,
Detroit.

Order to report to San Antonio revoked. Will keep you advised.

William.

Telegram

Rantoul, Illinois,
September 19, 1917.

Henry Russel,
Detroit.

Ordered to report Fort Wood, New York. Arrive there Saturday morning.

William.

Telegram

New York, N.Y.,
September 23, 1917.

Henry Russel,
Detroit.

Probably stationed Fort Wood, Bedloe's Island, for two weeks before sailing for France. Would like to see you.

William.

Telegram

New York, N.Y.,
Friday, October 5, 1917.

Henry Russel,
Detroit.

Honorably discharged as Sergeant today. First Lieutenant's commission dated September 20, 1917, received. Ordered to report Monday morning with personal and field equipment. Probably sail Tuesday.

William.

Interscription

My Dear Captain—

On December 4th, 1893, my brother George was persuaded to buy ten tickets to a lecture on astrology, the proceeds to be for some local charity. That evening the crowd of his boys, with their visiting friends, were making night hideous at his house, and to get rid of them, he asked if they would not like to go to the Opera House and see a show. They accepted with a shout, and he gave them the tickets, put up their carfares, and had a peaceful evening. He smiled to think what a bore the lecture on astrology would be to the boys.

The next morning at breakfast, he innocently inquired how they liked the show. To his surprise, they answered with great enthusiasm, "Bully. The lecturer had a magic lantern, and it was fine." A few minutes later, he remarked, "Do you know there is a new baby at Uncle Harry's house?" The boys exclaimed with great excitement, "When?" He answered, "Yesterday." They asked if he could tell the exact time the baby was born. That was a puzzler to him, and he asked why they wanted to know that.

They replied that the lecturer had said that he had cast the horoscope of the stars that day, and that the position of the constellations showed that on that very afternoon at about 5:20 o'clock, as near as he could calculate, a child was born—it may have been in Detroit and it may have been in Van Dieman's Land, but somewhere on earth—who would be the Columbus of aerial discovery. "Maybe," they said, "the baby at Uncle Harry's house is the very one."

The boys immediately adjourned to my house. I was alone at the breakfast table. Your friend Philip, who was the spokesman for the party, began by asking, "How is Aunt Nellie?" I was glad to report that she was very well. "And how is the baby boy?" He, too, seemed to be doing well. "There," said he to his companions, "I told you it was a boy"; and turning to me, "Now, Uncle Harry, we want to know just when that baby was born." I beat about the bush for further information as to the suitable time, and then left the table, walked up the front and down the back stairs, and told them I could not find out the exact minute, but as close as it could be figured it was just about 5:20 p. m. the day before, December 4th, 1893. The boys at once turned their backs on me. All talked at the same time, and settled it among themselves that there was no doubt but that the kid upstairs was the baby whose birth had been revealed to the astrologer. "But," they said, "we ought to tell you that the lecturer foretold that the aerial discoverer would lose his life by falling from a balloon before he was twenty-six years old."

You will remember, we talked about calling the baby "William Columbus," and the joke went so far that the relatives in Scotland thought that was his name, and you sent him a silver set, which he cherishes, marked "William Columbus Russel." Some of the family frequently use the nickname "Columbus," even though he was baptized in the memory of the good man, his grandfather, William Muir.

At that time, the aeroplane, now almost a vehicle, in common use, was a flight of fancy. Like Darius Green's flying machine, the world laughed at the thought of it. Years afterwards, a prominent American statesman was jeered at in Congress for introducing a measure to aid Professor Langley in the development of a flying craft, heavier than air. The great legislative body could not give attention to such foolishness, and the enthusiast, Langley, died without making any practical success of his experimental machine. The Wrights, who were boys then watching the birds in their flight, and other inventors have become the Columbuses of aerial discovery.

Nearly twenty-four years have slipped away, and William Muir Russel is now a First Lieutenant in the Aviation Section of the Signal Corps of the United States Army, and sails tomorrow with the Third Overseas Detachment for advanced training and active service. The enclosed touching poem, clipped from today's issue of *The Saturday Evening Post,* tells all my story. God, spare him to come back home again.

There is little chance of his going up in a balloon, but before he is twenty-six years of age, he will, no doubt, often be above the clouds in a far more dangerous pursuit. I am not superstitious, and attach no significance to the fiction of the astrologer's imaginative foreboding. The stars move on in their courses, fixed by the Eternal Ruler, and are guides to humanity, not controllers—to the least extent—of human life. The boys' adventure with the astrologer was merely a curious coincidence, such as is happening every day.

One cannot think, however, of the work of a birdman, especially in the terrible peril of war service, without a sinking of the heart, and yet—

I have grasped his hand—
Most men will understand—
And wished him, smiling, lucky chance
In France."

He graduated from Cornell last April, and immediately enlisted and was trained in the aviation fields of Memphis, Ashburn, and Rantoul. He seems to have passed all the tests satisfactorily, and has become an expert flyer.

His resemblance to his mother is so remarkable that you can picture what he looks like. I will send you his photograph, and am sure you will recall her dear face. He has always been an easy-going, care-free boy, with no fixed purpose except to be amiable and take things as they come. Five months, however, of soldier life, with only one day's leave at home, have made of him a serious man. The old time smile is gone, although some of his humour remains. He is completely engrossed in his work, and will talk of nothing but aero-dynamics, and the important part which aeroplanes will take in winning the victory for the Allies. He is a fluent writer, and like his grandfather, Muir, his handwriting is exceptionally fine. He has written long letters to me twice a week, and if ever published, they will be a real contribution to the history of this country's preparation for war. His enthusiasm is inspiring, and he is leaving home now for foreign service in this awful war like one who goes forth to joyous adventure.

It may be in the benevolence of Providence; it is well that his mother is not here to bear the parting. Eleanor, who has come to love him dearly, clings to him, and cannot say good-bye. Christine, too, has been in New York to see him off. He was ordered from Rantoul to report at New York for overseas service, without an opportunity to stop at Detroit, and so has had no farewells with Weeanne or Helen or the rest of the family. We have fitted him out the best we could with war equipment, personal comforts, and his Bible, Something from everyone in the family from his grandmother to the youngest kid, Weeanne's William, three weeks old (her fifth child, and my twelfth grandchild).

We are, therefore, only waiting here to give him the last word of God-speed, and I have occupied the time until he returns from Fort Wood this evening in putting my thoughts on paper in the way of this long letter to you. I feel, my dear captain, that you and the other friends and relatives across the sea will be interested, and trusting it will reach you and find you as happy as any of us can hope to be in these days of war and distress, I am as ever.

Affectionately yours,

Henry Russel.

To Captain Alex Ritchie,
St. John,
Ayr, Scotland.

I HAVE A SON
I have a son who goes to France
Tomorrow.
I have clasped his hand—
Most men will understand—
And wished him, smiling, lucky chance
In France.

My son!
At last the house is still—
Just the dog and I in the garden—dark—
Stars and my pipe's red spark—
The house his young heart used to fill
Is still.

He said, one day: "I've got to go
To France—Dad, you know how I feel!"
I knew. Like sun and steel
And morning. "Yes," I said; "I know
You'll go."

I'd waited just to hear him speak
Like that.
God, what if I had had
Another sort of lad.
Something too soft, too meek and weak

To speak!
And yet—
He could not guess the blow
He'd struck.
Why, he's my only son!
And we had just begun
To be dear friends. But I dared not show
The blow.

But now—tonight—
No, no; it's right;
I never had a righter thing
To bear. And men must fling
Themselves away in the grieving sight
Of right.

A handsome boy—but I, who knew
His spirit—well, they cannot mar
The cleanness of a star
That'll shine to me, always and true,
Who knew.

I've given him.
Yes; and had I more
I'd give them too— for there's a love
That asking asks above
The human measure of our store—
And more.

Yes; it hurts!
Here in the dark, alone—
No one to see my wet old eyes—
I'll watch the morning rise—
And only God shall hear my groan
Alone.

I have a son who goes to France
Tomorrow.
I have clasped his hand—
Most men will understand—
And wished him, smiling, lucky chance
In France.

— Emory Pottle.

ABOVE— S. S. *ST. LOUIS,* NEW YORK, OCTOBER 15, 1917
BELOW— AT SEA

Over There

U. S. M. S. *St. Louis,*
October 15, 1917.

Dear Father—

I am very comfortably located with Vanderhoef and Townes in a room on the starboard side. Have learned more or less of interior navigation, and familiarized myself with the inward ways of a ship on this, my first voyage at sea.

All the men in uniform have been kept below decks until we clear port, and so have not had a chance to say au revoir to the Statue of Liberty. Everything looks satisfactory so far, and I feel sure we will have a pleasant voyage. My address will be,

c/o Aviation Section,
American Expeditionary Forces,
Via New York.

Your loving son,

William.

Cablegram

Sans Origin,
Received October 28, 1917.

Henry Russel,
Detroit.

All right   William.

Dolphin Hotel,
Southampton, England,
October 25, 1917.

Dear Father—

Arrived safely after a beautiful trip across. Your prophecy of good weather was quite right except for one day when we were tossed about by a heavy wind.

I met some very interesting gentlemen. At our table sat a Major Cochrane of the Canadian Army, a friend of Enid Hendrie, and also a Mr. Delange, the inventor of a new thermo-telephone, which he said will revolutionize the telephone world. He told me that he was also the inventor of an instrument to telephone between an aeroplane in flight and the ground. He said he had been in the United States five months at the invitation of the government. He seemed to take a great fancy to me, and made himself numerous with our bunch. He gave us many unsolicited promises of assistance, if we should ever need it, in Europe.

Our quarters on the boat were comfortable, but not so elaborate as they pictured them to us before the start. However, it made little difference. We had no use for them except for sleep, and that came sure and sound. I am now stopping at this quaint hotel which I imagine is typical of England. It is much more homelike than ours. I was sorry that we were rushed from Liverpool directly here without stopping at London. I wanted to go there before crossing the Channel. To see England without London seems to me like Hamlet without the melancholy Dane.

Have just heard that this letter will go quickly if mailed at once. So am writing briefly and in haste.

Your loving son,

William.

November 6, 1917.

Dear Father—

I am here on the Continent after a trip across the sea without much incident. It is just what I wanted. I am not yet at the final destination, but expect to be within a day or two. This is an interesting world, and my time before actual work begins is taken up talking to English officers, watching the German prisoners, and seeing the country. One wearing the American uniform need not hesitate to talk with anybody. In fact, everybody comes smiling up to him first. The English officers are very interesting, and ready to do a favour. I haven't had the good fortune yet of making the acquaintance of many of the French officers with whom I shall be associated, nor have I had an opportunity to visit Mr. Sharp, but have already seen many old familiar faces.

Orders now made require me to retrace part of my steps. I am glad to find that the new duties will not interfere with my advanced training. I will have charge of aeroplanes and motors in one of the larger flying fields.

When once definitely settled, my letters will be more frequent, but short and rather indefinite on account of censorship.

Your loving son,

William.

November 8, 1917.

Dear Father—

I have retraced none of my footsteps. Still on the Continent. My work is mostly clerical, and will be until the school for advanced training opens in a short time. Every afternoon, I go to a field. Villa Coubley, where we have a few aeroplanes for the men in the building where I am, and so keep my hand in the game. I have also learned to fly with the stick control, which is quite different from the Dep which I flew in the States. The machines in use here are beautiful. The hours of work are nine to twelve and two to six—the entire afternoon at the field. More familiar faces turn up every day. It is very gratifying, as only four of our original bunch are left here.

I can get along quite well now in French so far as speaking to another goes, but unless they talk to me slowly, I am lost. Am building up my vocabulary and learning the expressions of the day reading French newspapers.

Comfort and the best of health have been mine ever since we parted in New York.

Love to all,

Your loving son,

William.

November 12, 1917.

Dear Father—

Not a word yet from anybody at home, and I am wondering whether you have heard from me. The mail is still in confusion, and a fellow is fortunate to get a letter. However, they are working out a good system, and I think the trouble will be remedied before long. My location is still on the continent, and I am busy all mornings on a temporary job from which I will be relieved as soon as my flying orders come through. Every afternoon, I take a beautiful automobile drive to Villa Coubley, where there are all types of machines, and I am having fine times flying all by myself. The very first day, Lieutenant Chatain

142

gave me fifteen minutes' instruction with the stick control—the first time I had ever used it—and as I seemed to get the knack of it he told me to go ahead, that I was all right.

It was one of the well-known Nieuport machines, and the best way I can explain the difference between our machines and it, is to compare our original curved dash Oldsmobile with a Packard twin-six. The Nieuport has a powerful motor and a light fuselage, and will pull you anywhere at any angle. It avoids a lot of the danger which was so common in the Curtis. Outside of the quick response to the controls, the great difference is in the terrific speed at which you take off the ground and make your landing.

One objectionable feature of the flying at this season is the intense cold. You cannot imagine how bitter it is. I put on a couple of knitted masks, then Allen's leather fur-lined helmet and my goggles. Even then, the part of my face which is exposed stiffens and prevents me from moving my mouth. My hands also become numb with the cold. I usually go up for twenty minutes at a time, and then hug a stove for a while before trying it again.

At breakfast the other morning, an elderly gentleman drew up beside me, and asked many questions about the States. He introduced himself as Mr. Wilbur, Consul General at Genoa, and was very agreeable. He was here getting a passport into Switzerland to bring away his wife and child who were living there. He had met Doctors Torrey and McLean of Detroit, and was very optimistic about the Italian situation.

Last night I dined with a Mr. Mitchell who had an immense stable before the war, and who has many interests in Russia. His descriptions are very vivid and thrilling. He has invited us to dine with him on the 14th again, and we are looking forward to it as a treat.

I have discovered that I have bought a great deal of unsatisfactory wardrobe, and if I could make my purchases again, could do so to great advantage. Tell anybody coming over to bring warm clothing without regard to looks. Anything will do if it is warm. The high hunting boots you forced on me are about the most useful things in my equipment. Rain, rain and mud are incessant. English woollen clothing seems to be better and cheaper. Heavy uniforms are the thing. At the same time, one should have as little baggage as practicable, as you have to handle it yourself, and it has a habit of getting lost.

Am well. Love to all.

Your loving son,

William.

15 METRE NIEUPORT PURSUIT PLANE (AVION DE CHASSE)

November 16, 1917.

Dear Father—

I have moved into a very attractive little apartment with three nice fellows; new friends I have made. Our apartment is costing us ten *francs* a day, and our three meals eighteen *francs*. We have two double bedrooms, and an intervening sitting room and bath. Right across the way is Fouquet's Restaurant. Whenever we feel rich, which is not often, we dine there.

I have heard from some of the other boys who came over in the same ship, and fear that they are not as well fixed as I am.

Every afternoon, weather permitting, and more often not, I go out and fly, so that I am getting a pretty good training on my own initiative. I have come to feel at home and to enjoy the sensation of sailing through the air as much as on the heavy rigged Curtis at Rantoul.

I have no letters from you yet, nor have I had a word from Maury. I am not alone in being without news from home and therefore have not felt disappointed.

The other day we hired a worthy old sea-going hack to see whatever sights of Paris might be open. In the Invalides' Court, Guynemer's aeroplane has been set up, and when an officer approaches it, he salutes, as we did, but the women kiss it. He is one of the great heroic figures of France at present. The rest of the sights now are, as you recall them—Arc de Triomphe, Madeleine, Notre Dame, Eiffel Tower, etc. The night life, I presume, is far different from what you remember it. The restaurants close at 9:30 sharp, and you must leave at that time whether you have finished dinner or not. Dancing is absolutely prohibited, and there is no music except at the theatres. I have been to several of the French theatres. As yet, the talk is too fast for me to catch on. Their take-offs on the American soldiers and sailors are very good, and no show is complete without it.

Two things I want—one is cigarettes, and the other is more knitted helmets. The ones I brought were fine, but I gave all but one away. They are most essential. The cold is terrific at any altitude, and I have never flown here yet unless a part of the time in a fog or heavy mist.

As you remember, I was in very good health in New York, and I am glad to report that I was better in England, and best in France. Hoping that you are all as well as I am,

Your loving son,

William.

November 24, 1917.

Dear Father—

Just a line to keep in touch with you and let you know something of my whereabouts.

More familiar faces appear each day. Yesterday, perhaps, might be called "Detroit Reunion Day." On the way to the Headquarters Building, where I work mornings, I was delighted to run across Colonel Hutton. He was surprised to find me in Paris as a commissioned officer. He said it only seemed a couple of weeks since he was helping to put through my enlistment at Washington.

While we were talking, Mr. Dayton of Detroit came along, and shortly afterwards, a government automobile drove up, and out stepped Mr. Angus Smith and Herbert Hughes. Both are at work in Headquarters in the same building as I am. Theirs are permanent jobs, however. Praise the Lord, mine is not, but it has been a good experience, and I have been able to learn much of the important work of supplying an army, and of military organisation, which, if I should ever have a command may mean much to me. It has also brought me into intimate contact with my superior officers. What I will be doing next no one can say—so many various duties have been hinted at.

Last night Vallie came to the apartment, and we dined with Miss Hoeveler, Bill's sister. Vallie did not enlist as a private in the army when the government took over the ambulance corps, and now goes to Italy to serve in the ambulance corps there. Many of the young men who were in the ambulance corps are in a rather uncomfortable predicament. The United States government is forcing them to enlist as privates, or sending them back to the States to be drafted.

My flying, although still carried on independently, seems to be progressing well. I have had a chance to associate with expert French lieutenants, who are only too glad to give an American any information and advice they can. They tell me what to do, and then correct where I fail in my efforts. In this way, I am getting on to all the necessary stunts which later will be required. A good deal of the flying must be carried on quite near the ground, as the weather at this time is very foggy, and the clouds are low. It is the more difficult kind of flying. It is more and more fascinating as the time goes on and I become more proficient.

Am in perfect health. Love to all,

Your loving son,

William.

St. Nazaire, France,
December 1, 1917.

Dear Father—

I have been fortunate enough to be sent on a trip from headquarters through one of the most beautiful sections of France, along the Loire River, through the valley and *château* district between Tours and Nantes. It was Thanksgiving Day, but the only feasting I did was on the scenery. Although at the end of November, the country seemed as green as I imagine it would be in mid-summer. On the hills along the valley are built beautiful white *châteaux*—little villas and great castles. St. Nazaire is a curious French seaport town. My job was to bring forty-five Packard three-ton trucks, fifteen trailers, and ten gasoline tank trucks from St. Nazaire to Paris. It was quite a job to quarter fifty-five men and ration them in strange little towns along the route, some three hundred miles, with my diminutive knowledge of French. To obtain parking space for the trucks is always a problem. I have a perfectly good six cylinder Hudson for myself, which I am also to take back to Paris.

Sandy Wetherbee of Detroit has gone into the bombing end of aviation, and is taking his training. The other four of us. Bill Hoeveler, Vanderhoef, Joe Trees, and I are for pursuit work. Not sure yet that our hopes will be gratified, but we are under the instruction of a French lieutenant to fit us for that line of service.

The other night, I had the great pleasure of dining with Raoul Lufberry. The story of his experiences was thrilling, and his advice worthwhile. Ed. Buford had a nasty fall the other day. He broke his shoulder and sustained other minor injuries about the head. He is getting the best of attention, however, at a good hospital, and has nothing to complain of. It saves him a lot of work and worry.

Herbert Hughes will return to Detroit soon, and I have asked him to make a personal report. I think it will relieve any anxiety that you may have about me for a while at any rate.

I met one of my Cornell friends here the other day, and wondered whether it were possible that you would prefer to have me out of harm's way as he is. He has a beautiful bomb-proof job, and has social work to do. He resides in a fine apartment, and has time to strut about the various tea rooms, which he does with much swagger. Vallie and I were proud to be recognised. The time may come when I may wish that I had his job, as things look dark over here—more so, it seems, than they do to you in America. The war will surely last a long time yet, and the aviation service will have to do a great part. You need have no doubt but that it will be performed, whatever it may cost in life and suffering.

I am comforting myself with the belief that you are all well, because, as yet, I have received not a word from home. My only mail has been letters from other boys over here.

Am in the best of health.

Your loving son,

William.

St. Nazaire, France,
December 4, 1917.

Dear Father—

I am still here gathering aviation material for my auto train. You would be surprised at the amount. It hardly seems that submarines can be accomplishing anything to see the ships coming in in large convoys, and the forest of masts in this newly built seaport, a beautiful sight.

Today, after I had left my men to keep tab on the checkers who note aviation boxes and their destination, I went aboard one of the warships on which I understood some of my material was loaded. Among the ship's officers, I met a boy in naval uniform who looked good to me. He hailed me with the greeting, "Isn't this Bill Russel?" It was Louis Carr, of St. Louis, a classmate whom I had not seen since the Hill school days. He invited me to lunch on the ship, and gave me the first real American meal I have eaten since I left you in New York,

Most of the work done on the docks is by German prisoners—big strong fellows, probably the first to enter the war. It makes me curious to know what their thoughts must be, unloading unlimited supplies from an undrained country. The effect on the French people is apparent. There is no room for doubt; it is a mighty stimulus.

My birthday was celebrated in a fine little French restaurant here, and Lieutenant Reilly was my only guest. It was a pleasant but short evening. At 9:30, we were invited to leave the cafe, and be off the streets or spend the night in the cooler at the request of the military police.

The marines are the police, and we know that they do their work effectively.

I am looking forward to my trip back to Paris through one of the prettiest parts of France. I will have to drive slowly on account of keeping with the trucks, and it will give me a splendid chance to see a lovely part of the world. I shall be glad to get back to Paris because there is no flying field near here, so that even in the leisure hours during the gathering of my freight, I cannot take wings. There may be a chance to go up in a dirigible from a big station located near, possibly tomorrow.

I have told more in this letter than usual, but don't think I have given away any secrets. It is a pleasure to write to you, as it seems as if I were having a visit and talk with you.

Give a good word to all.

Your loving son,

William.

St. Nazaire, France,
December 6, 1917.

Dear Father—

A great opportunity has come to write you a letter in more detail than I have yet done, so I am going to rehearse some of the past. Am sending this letter direct on an American ship.

On leaving New York, October 15th last, we were rushed below deck until port was cleared, after which we were allowed to come above. Instead of the long roundabout route for sailing, our ship made a dash straight across the ocean, not picking up any convoys until the danger zone was reached, when two American destroyers took us into Liverpool on the night of the seventh day. Our quarters on the ship were comfortable, our meals excellent, and the portions liberal compared with army rations. It was a pleasant trip with beautiful weather.

We disembarked at Liverpool in the morning, and were immediately rushed through to Southampton and put up at a comfortable little English hotel.

After one day without any signs of orders, some of us got leave to go to London. We were met at the station by men of the Royal Flying Corps. They were very hospitable, and took us at once in an automobile through the gloomy streets of the darkened city to the flying field. One of the staff aeroplanes was turned over to our disposal, and I was taken up in some of their latest machines, including one of the new German Albatrosses, a wonderful machine, the leading plane of the day. I had an opportunity to experience all their stunts as a passenger, and in the course of the flight, by the register, reached a maximum speed of one hundred and thirty-eight miles an hour.

My first real sight of London was a bird's-eye view from thousands of feet up in the air.

Returning to Southampton, we found a transport awaiting us, and perhaps the worst night of my existence ahead. We were crowded into a small boat about ten o'clock that evening, and everybody was ordered to put on a life preserver. It was a beautiful moonlight night, and for that reason, they hesitated to send us over, but finally decided to make a dash, even though it was as bright as day. The boat was cleared of all cabins and chairs, and we sat around on the deck. All lights were extinguished, and smoking prohibited. The excitement was intense, and everybody on the *qui vive*. It was several hours' run to La Havre and the Channel was active. At 3:30 in the morning, we hove into sight of France.

As we slid into the harbour, day was breaking, and it was a beautiful sight to see the sun and land. We were immediately marched to an English rest camp, and got there just too late for breakfast. There were no orders for us, so we settled down to make the best of it. Our quarters were in an old horse-shed which was temporarily fixed up with bars and cross wires for mattresses. Our bed rolls were still on board, so the first evening they gave us two blankets apiece, and bade us goodnight. It was very cold all the time we were there, and each morning was as welcome as the first.

After five days of this, orders came from headquarters to go to Paris. The long-hoped-for day arrived. We were roughly awakened at four o'clock in the morning, and at six, were on the way. There are few signs of war in this part of France except for the many uniforms and the train loads of supplies. Towards evening, we arrived and reported at aviation headquarters and to the provost marshal. Paris was fascinating—nearly everybody in some type of uniform, and nearly all ornamented with many coloured decorations. The restaurants and hotels resemble the chorus in a musical comedy with its various colours and costumes. The English do not wear medals, merely a little piece of ribbon.

The French pay most cordial attention to the United States uniform, and everyone who can speak English greets and entertains you. It is strangely pathetic to hear the stories from the front, and you realise at once what a salvation our declaration of war has been to this people. I have, of course, gained much first-hand knowledge from conversations with French and English officers, and have ideas concerning the war which never entered my mind until now. You cannot but feel intensely bitter, and actually cherish your hatred and are completely absorbed with the one purpose to fit yourself to do your part in crushing such a cruel and relentless foe.

You know generally my experiences and duties since I was fortunate enough to be picked out to come to St. Nazaire. At headquarters, I was thrown into close contact with the supply end, and came to realise more fully the great undertaking of the war. This trip has been still more of a lesson, since I have had the chance to see the ships coming in from the States with their vast supplies.

The road to Paris by which I will return, lies in the *château* country. We will pass through Angers, Nantes, LaFleche, LeMans, Nogent-le-Rotrou, Chartres, Versailles, and then Paris. It sounds like a pleasure jaunt. What will be in store for me after that is very indefinite. I hope to go at once to a perfection school established well up towards the front, to which thirty men will be sent for rapid advanced training on speed scout machines.

I have been in perfect health ever since my departure, but no letters yet from the States.

Your loving son,

William.

St. Nazaire, France,
December 16, 1917.

Dear Father—

Another interesting trip, which accounts for the length of time between letters.

Monday I started for a little French town called St. Mairent with six Packard trucks and thirteen men. The route lay through a beautiful part of France, and the good roads stretched out for miles before us. It was aggravating to travel at only twelve miles an hour over such marvellous roads, but after a long patient ride, at the end of the day, we came to a strange little French town called Chatillon amid cheers of "*Vive l'Amerique.*" It was not hard to tell that we were the first American soldiers here, and it was a simple matter to obtain quarters for my men; and for myself, the most distinguished gentleman in town, M. Louis Ferez, inquired for the commanding officer. He was a refugee from Lille, and had established an excellent shoe shop here until he might return to his home. He took me to his house, and put me into a beautifully furnished room, one of the few warm spots in France.

Needless to say, I was nearly frozen after driving all day in the open,

151

perched up on the top of a truck on the tenth day of December. A very charming family gathered at dinner. It was excellent, but most embarrassing to me. Mother and father and the young ladies jabbered French at me, and I know nearly all were questions. After dinner, it was better. They talked slower and got out a *Learn English Over Night* book, with which we had great fun and an intelligible conversation. I was really pleased to find that I could understand French and make myself understood so well, but must admit, they encouraged and helped conversation.

Early the next morning, I bade them *adieu* and started again through the beautiful country, and at lunch time drew into Bressuire with two trucks dead on the end of a tow line, dry of gasoline. Gasoline has gone beyond being scarce; it is impossible to buy it. The French military authorities politely said they would spare me some if I insisted, but urged me to get it elsewhere. I then was able to find a long distance telephone, and was told to wait about four hours. I started to spend the time visiting the ruins of an old *château* which I spotted on the way, and was stopped by an elderly lady, who asked me in good English if I were an American. She took me to her house, the finest in the town, for tea. It was a beautiful white stone villa, and the old lady and her daughter and some guests plied me with questions about America.

At five o'clock, I returned to the trucks, got the men fed heartily, and started out for a night trip. At 2:30 in the morning, we reached our destination, nearly frozen and starved. Again we were unexpected, and ushered into a cold dismal barracks to spend the remainder of the night. In the early morning, I had the men go over every truck before turning them over to the major for inspection, and then came back here by rail. I sat up all night and changed cars four times. Tomorrow—back for Paris.

I have been away from headquarters since Thanksgiving Day, and shall be disappointed if I do not find a letter on my return.

Your loving son,

William.

Aviation Section,
A. E. F., France,
December 25, 1917.

Dear Father—

I have taken the chance of sending to you all, whom I have in constant thought, a small present, which, on account of its convenient shape, I thought I might ask Miss Hoeveler to carry.

This present means more to me than any other which I have ever had the pleasure of giving, and I feel that it will be received in the same spirit.

In the first place, these handkerchiefs were made by a woman, at least the monograms, who was once moderately well off; but, through the great casualty of war, has been forced to eke out whatever small living she can in this manner. Her personal loss has been a husband, a son, and three brothers. In the next place, they were purchased with money which is the first that I feel I have ever really earned—maybe not yet, but will in the future.

Through the unforeseen happenings since last Christmas, I have been made to realise the true meaning and feeling of this day. It is the first Christmas that I have ever been separated from those whom I love, and instead of being a day of festivity, it has changed to a day of thought, and one that will linger in my memory for years, if I am spared. I have had the same isolated feeling on two other days in my life, and yet, at the same time, it is one of closer reunion. It is a great consolation to me, although at the same time I am sorry to think that the greater hardship falls upon you at home, who, in your doubt, are worrying about us.

This thought is uppermost in my mind, and when the time for trial shall come, I am sure it will be a stimulus, and will bring out the best that is in me; it may be meagre, but it will at least be my share, and I hope that it will not be a disappointment.

With these small gifts to you all, I send my love and all good wishes for a Merry Christmas, as well as for a brighter New Year and a happy reunion hereafter. Give my fondest remembrances to all who are dear to me.

Your loving son,

William.

A. E. F., France,
December 27, 1917.

Dear Father—

I have just returned from an eventful trip, which was a wonderful experience, but terribly hard work. From St. Nazaire to Paris is a matter of three hundred miles, and as fate would have it, all the elements worked against us. We started a week ago last Sunday noon in a blinding, soaking rain storm, and at our first stop found rather poor quarters at an American Base Hospital. Here I was forced to leave two of my men with bad colds. This left me one short, and I had to give up my Hudson car and drive a truck myself. The next three days we met heavy snow storms. The trucks would come to a hill, the wheels would spin and get no traction, and we had to take them over one by one. They were too heavily loaded. Meantime, some of the boys would be letting their motors run in order to make the dash, and so our gasoline was used up, and you cannot buy a drop.

At Le Mans, I was up against it. The French people gathered about were asking me a thousand questions, so I asked a few in return, and found that a Belgian camp was located near there, and the colonel, through an interpreter, heard my story and gave me five hundred litres of gasoline. I was again forced to get more at a large French flying school. So the troubles went on, and just one week later, I arrived in Paris with all my trucks—thirty-two Packards, thirty Fords and fifteen trailers. I had stopped one day to have the boys go over the motors. It looked mighty good to see the long line draw up before headquarters where all the big men were stationed, with every motor in fine running order. The weather was continuously bad, bitter cold all the time, either hail or snow after the first day. The men complained a little at first, but when I left my fine touring car and drove a truck myself everyone stopped grumbling.

On arriving at Paris, I put ten men in the hospital with grippe, I am stuffed up somewhat myself with a cold in the head. I was anxious about getting here for Christmas, and by plugging along forty or fifty miles a day we reached here on the 23rd. I was delighted to find a big bunch of mail waiting, the first from home. Christmas we spent quietly. In the evening we were invited to a Christmas gathering and to an elegant dinner at an American gentleman's.

Today Joe Trees, who has been living with us, received orders to go to London to take charge of the personnel in the aviation section. It is a good job, and an opportunity for advancement. He will get plenty of flying at the English schools. My own flying has, of course, been held up by my trip, but I am at it again now, and can handle the Spad as well as the Nieuport. The Spad is the finest little thing imaginable; seemingly fragile, but I think it is stronger than a Nieuport.

I find that I will be sent within the next week to conduct an auto truck train of aeroplane material to the front. It will, of course, be interesting, but takes me away once more from what I want. The commanding officer has asked me to transfer from aviation to the transportation department with suggestion of a promotion. I refused so blankly that I am afraid I hurt his feelings, which I regret. He is to have charge of all the United States automobiles in France, and is a very competent officer.

Your loving son,

William.

Aviation Section,
A. E. F., France,
January 7, 1918.

Dear Father—

Christmas and New Years have passed, and I must confess it is a sort of relief to have them over. Although both were happy days in so far as the hospitality and very kind treatment by friends went, yet there was an indescribable lonesomeness which made them strange.

We have now dipped into the new year, and feel that brighter things will come with it. The help from America will surely make itself felt, and the fact that so many of our troops are here with so many more to come eager to fight and do their part is the only sunshine breaking through the dark clouds which still overhang this unfortunate country. The French are so down to bone and sinew, and have so little physical strength left that it seems to me not so much a matter of the moral effect of American intervention, although that cannot be overlooked, but it is the actual fighting force we can give, and the willingness to fight with them and alongside of them against a common cruel enemy.

And yet, of course, there is great anxiety as to what the late winter and early spring may bring. We may have to meet troubles and disasters, but now that the A. E. F. are in it, there is never a doubt but that we will win.

My Christmas, away from home in a foreign land at war, was as pleasant as could be expected under the circumstances. Mrs. Halley Smith and Mr. and Mrs. Hood were very thoughtful and kind, and your fine letters and boxes came just in the nick of time. So far, I have had only two letters from you, the last dated November 16th. Yesterday, Ambassador Sharp was kind enough to call and deliver to me your telegram.

Since my letter of the day after Christmas, I have had another trip, even more interesting than the two former ones. If it had not been for

155

the terrific cold, it would have been as enjoyable as it was of interest every minute. It was my first visit to the front. I do not mean the first line trenches, but near enough so that I could hear the continual roar of our own artillery, and see the bursting shells of the enemy, and the Allied planes in their reconnaissance work.

Without glasses, they look like mere dots, and an amateur cannot tell the friendly from the hostile. It was an impressive sight, and it is hard to believe that such harmless looking specks in the sky can be made instruments of so much help and so much destruction. I had a chance to see a good bit of the country, and passed through towns which have been practically obliterated by the artillery and aviation fire of former battles.

Now I am returning to my former situation, and find a new job awaiting, which keeps me busy in the mornings. Afternoons are free, and I spend all the time flying—to Villa Coubley as usual, first a little work on the machine and then into the air. Aeroplanes are becoming attached to my life as companions and pets. There are two kinds in particular, the Nieuport and the Spad, which I alternate in flying, and if I get out early enough, take a flight in each. It may seem inconceivable to you—sometimes it does to me—but now I think no more of it than driving an automobile. Even if the novelty has worn off, there is a continuous pleasure. It reminds me of golf in that there is so much to learn, and you always have the feeling that you can do better in your next flight. Hope springs eternal in an aviator's breast. Twice, I have flown high over Paris. It is a wonderful sight to see the straight avenues radiating from the Arc d' Etoile, and to see the parks like dabs in the midst of a vast city. Now, I have had a bird's-eye view of London and Paris. I wonder what next.

I have a world of interesting stories to tell, which I have gathered from the many people in all the walks of home and military life I am constantly meeting. Someday, if I am spared, I can tell them by the fireside.

Thank Mrs. Campbell, George B., Anne, Helen, Christine, and Aunt Jennie for all their remembrances; letters also from Eleanor and Weeanne. I will write everybody the first chance I get, but now, in the evenings of my busy days, I am very tired. You would entirely approve my habits—early to bed and . . . .

Love to you and Eleanor and all the rest. Am well.

Your loving son,

William.

A. E. F., France,
January 14, 1918.

Dear Father—

Boxes by the score have been coming, and believe me, they are appreciated. A very nice package came from Allen and Christine, and one which made me laugh and cry from dear old Smut (Ward Smith of Virginia). Letters, though, do not yet come regularly. I have received only very few of the many which must have been written, but one cannot complain considering the short time the system has been established for the scattered soldiers' mail, and the great confusion that was caused when all the Christmas packages arrived just as the new mailing system was put into effect.

I have not told you before, on purpose, that one of my steamer trunks was lost at Southampton. Only yesterday word came from the quartermaster that it had been found. It contained, of course, all the things that I wanted most—all my warm flying clothes—and so what I couldn't draw from the quartermaster I have had to do without.

I was surprised and delighted the other day to be informed that I will probably be sent to England to attend, with four of the other boys, an aerial gunnery school. The course will last about four weeks, then to a perfection school for two weeks. On finishing the latter course, the men are fully trained and held in readiness for use "somewhere." I understand my name is on the list, and the minute I hear definitely, I will cable you and let you know as much as the censor will permit. The trip across the Channel under present conditions is terrible, but I will be glad to go to England. Maybe I will have a chance to fly across. The British Royal Flying Corps sets the pace for training and getting a flyer into active, useful service at the front.

I have had a splendid opportunity to see the cities and the country and the different people in each throughout France. My impressions are as various as the localities. The people in the country places, like our friends in lower Canada, seem, from our American point of view, merely to exist, and yet appear to be satisfied. I sometimes think that they are the happier. One visiting the country south of Paris would hardly know there was a war, except that so many of the men and older boys are absent. One discomfort I have never escaped so far is the dreadful cold. Mufflers and rubbers are constantly worn. There is, of course, a great scarcity of wood and coal. Food, on the other hand, seems to be plentiful and good—all except the concoction known as war bread, which is a constant reminder of war.

It is amusing now for me to think of the things of which we used to complain. Talk about the telephone—if you cannot get a chance to use one installed by our Signal Corps, you do without it. The real aristocracy of Paris now are the taxicab drivers. They are given a certain allowance of gasoline per week, and it makes the drivers so proud that only if you happen to be going in the direction in which the taxi is headed, and in which the driver desires to go, and are not going too far, will he carry you. Otherwise you can walk; and the walking is good in Paris.

Except possibly for the morals of an American in uniform, the Yankee soldier clothes are surely a valuable drawing card here. If they can only be as repulsive to the Germans as they are attractive to the French, we will win the war very soon, but do not overlook one thing which will help to bring it about—France is a brave nation, and has done its share, and will yet do more.

Love to all,

Your loving son,

William.

A. E. F., France,
January 25, 1918.

Dear Father—

Life for me continues one of comfort rather than of strife. My work is still in the vicinity of Paris, and although it is very strenuous, with long hours, I can look forward to my comfortable room in the evening. I am able now only to have two afternoons and Sunday off for flying, but it is not so essential as before, because my instruction is practically at an end. I have not, however, yet had the training in aerial gunnery, but this is only a matter of a three weeks' course, and I am expecting orders any day to report at that school.

All the acrobatics and squadron flying, really the two most difficult phases of aerial work, are completed. The acrobatics consist of three stunts which sound impossible in description, and which would draw a thousand dollars a flight in exhibition at a side show, but in these machines (Spads) are not so much.

The first is a vertical spiral with the motor cut off and a continual bank of 90°. It is very difficult to keep your spirals even and to keep your machine in a vertical position.

The second is the side-slip, and is most valuable in fighting, as it is the quickest way to get away from the enemy if he gains the superior position on you. In this, you place your machine in a vertical bank and allow her to fall vertically towards the ground off on one side. In this way, you can lose about three thousand feet in less than one minute. It is much faster than the vertical nose dive.

The third, which is really beautiful, and looks very difficult, but is not, is what the French call the *renversement*. This is also very valuable in fighting, as it is the quickest way to turn when being pursued by the enemy. While flying along level, you suddenly pull the nose up into the air, let her slip to one side over on her back, then nose her to the ground and come out going in the opposite direction. All of these movements in five seconds. It seems most complicated, but it is necessary for you to learn it in forty-five minutes. You practice the movement on the ground for some time before you go up, and then you try it. Many get into the *vrille*, or tail spin, the first few times until they finally get it. It is very pretty to watch, and the sensations at first are quite unpleasant; later you do not mind it at all. The remarkable part is that no altitude is lost in the entire operation. You may understand it better from my rough pen and ink sketches.

This must sound like a month's training, but at the end of three days on the acrobatic field, you are doing them all. So much for flying.

The other night, Harry Colburn, who is here temporarily from Lyon, and I went to see a good show. A great deal of it was English; in fact, most of the songs. They had an American Jazz band, which is the hit of the show. The French people simply go wild over it.

Last night, I had dinner at the Restaurant Tour D 'Argent which we were told is the oldest restaurant in Paris. In the evening, Lieutenants Ormsby, Colburn, Schuyler and I played bridge. Tonight, I am going to call on Ambassador Sharp. It is really the first opportunity which I have had.

Everything is very uncertain at present. There are many rumours concerning the spring and what it will bring with it. Everybody is in doubt. I have not the faintest idea of what my movements will be. However, I feel confident that definite orders will arrive for me soon, having been told that my present job is only temporary. As long as this lasts, you have no need to worry about my safety and comfort. I have everything that one could wish.

My mail from the States is very uncertain. I have heard nothing from any of you for nearly a month. One must satisfy himself over here that "no news is good news," or you are seldom in a satisfied frame of mind.

Top.
Flying Towards you.

Top.
Flying Towards you and upwards.

Flying downwards towards you.

Top.
Flying Towards you.

Top.
Flying Towards you.

Top.
Flying away from you.

Bottom.
Upsidedown.
Flying Towards you.

Bottom.
Upsidedown. Flying Towards you but downwards.

Pen and Ink Sketch of *reinforcement* in body of letter

Hoping that you are well and happy, and that the deprivations of war are being accepted willingly, as I judge from the papers that you are suffering more than we are from them, I remain with love to all,

Your loving son,

William.

A. E. F., France,
January 28, 1918.

Dear Father—

Your letter of December 17th, with its Christmas greeting, has just come, and I had to blush as I read of your feelings and your sympathy. I have more comforts than I am entitled to, and if you all had been with me, my Christmas would have been indeed a merry one. As I wrote, your welcome boxes arrived in perfect time, and Mrs. Hood and Mrs. Halley-Smith took us three into their homes in the kindest holiday spirit.

Your letter speaking of the numerous accidents in the States makes one think, but I can assure you that if traced to their source, it will be found that the principal cause is carelessness. We have had four bad accidents here, and all of them were due either to carelessness or lack of skill, which can be traced back to carelessness, in letting an inexperienced flyer assume too much. Two of the accidents last Saturday were unnecessary, and an exhibition of how not to fly. Both the boys got out miraculously well—no bones broken nor internal injuries. One of them, while he is just as good as he was before, will have a different face, and may have to introduce himself to former friends.

As I continue with my work, my confidence becomes greater, and I feel sure that it is, making some allowances, as safe as any other pursuit in war. When I talk with other young men who have really done something, I feel like an *embusqué*. They are all so enthusiastic about flying, and their casualties have been so few. In fact, the French infantry look upon their flyers as *embusqués*. This ought to be a comfort to you, even if it is a reflection on me.

I forgot to tell you that we have electrically heated fur combination suits, helmets and shoes. The wires run inside the lining, and the electricity is generated from a little motor with a propeller set out on one wing of the aeroplane. The air current caused by the speed rotates the propeller of the motor, thus generating the electricity.

The pictures from home were like a reunion. I brought your picture and mother's, and am sorry I have not the rest. I realise now how much I would appreciate them, as I feel sure that it will be a long time before I will be able to return and see any of you. At times, the prospects are bright, and then again the outlook, while, of course, not hopeless, is gloomy. Some of the Lafayette Esquadrille boys with whom I have been playing around, tell me that the feeling at the front has decidedly changed in the last month. They are sure that it will be a bad spring, a big German offensive and severe fighting. We will have to go through it before the backbone of the enemy is broken, and it will take our help—after that, calmer sailing. The British feel the same way, terrible work this spring, and the worst will be over.

Now, too, the Russians seem to be coming into their own again, and will not allow the Germans to bulldoze them. I sincerely hope they will continue to be a thorn in Germany's eastern side.

Last week, the bunch of us made the rounds of the interesting restaurants in Paris. Each gave a dinner for the others at the different places, Veil's, LaRue, Giro's, Henri's, and Tour d'Argent. The last, said to be the oldest restaurant in Paris, I like best. Pressed duck, with elaborate procedure at the large centre table, similar to the way our fine red-heads are squeezed and served at the Detroit Club, was the *piece de resistance* of my menu.

Hastily yours. With love to all. Am well.

Your loving son,

William.

A. E, F, France,
February 2, 1918.

Dear Father—

I have had a great experience since my last letter to you. Although it had been rumoured for several weeks, the air raid on Paris the other night took everybody by surprise. I think that it was not really expected, and now that the heathenish thing has happened, the feeling of hatred and indignation is intense.

I had been down town for supper, and afterwards to the Theatre Collisée on the Champs Elysees. As we left the theatre, we spoke of the beauty of the evening. The sky was filled with stars, and there was a beautiful full moon, and somebody remarked that it was the kind of a night to raid Paris. Several evenings before, I had called on Ambassador Sharp, and he had said that he did not believe that Paris would be raided until after Germany had made further peace offerings. I told this to the boys, and we concluded he must be right, and dismissed the

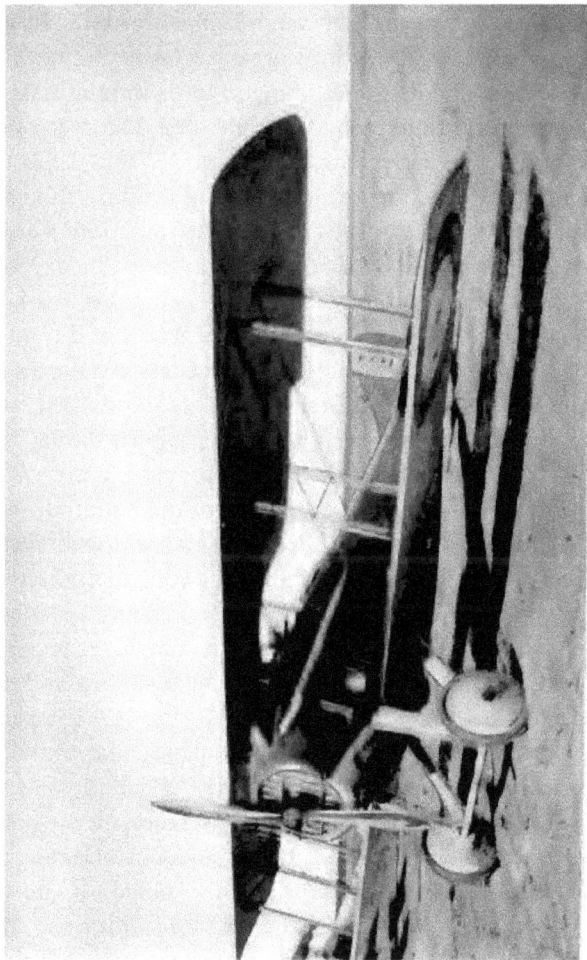

Spad Pursuit Plane, 180 hp., (Avion de chasse) One Vicker's Gun

thought of a raid from our minds. A short time afterwards, when we were sitting around talking about anything but air raids, the warning siren sounded twice. It was notice of an oncoming raid. We immediately extinguished all the lights and went out on the balcony. Fire engines rushed through the streets sending warnings additional to the two blasts of the siren. There was little confusion on the streets, although people and taxis did not wander aimlessly about. It was about the same rush you would see on Wall Street during the noon hour.

We waited for the next development, and a kind of sickly feeling came over me, due, I think, to utter helplessness. This was soon driven away by the intense excitement, and the noise of aeroplanes, guns and bombs. This, sometime, might be my line of action, I thought, and I soon calmed down, and looked on with the intention of learning as much as I could from my poor post of observation. The motors of the French planes could be heard distinctly in their patrol work over the city. In the distance, we could hear the sharp crack of the anti-aircraft guns, and this cleared any doubt that the raiders were really coming. Then came the sound of the German motors and the red, white and green lights of the French machines could be seen flitting across the sky. The accompanying danger was next brought more vividly to our minds by the hollow sounding explosion of the bombs dropping every few minutes. This lasted for fifteen minutes, and again the city was quiet except for the hum of the French motors, an entirely different sound from the German motor.

About twenty minutes later, the anti-aircraft guns again announced an approach. Many coloured signal lights could be seen, and the thundering of guns lasted for half an hour. During this last period, the German machines could not be seen, but from the sound of their motors (it was easy to distinguish them), we judged them to be about six thousand feet in the air. The French machines, on the other hand, were visible nearly all the time, and flew at about one thousand feet. While we were watching, the sky suddenly lighted up, and we saw a machine fall enveloped in flames. The next day, we learned that it was a German machine of the Gotha II type. One of our machines, in endeavouring to make a forced landing in the Place de la Concorde, struck an unlighted iron electric light post, and both pilot and observer lost their lives. It was wonderful to watch the French machines signalling to one another, and at the same time receiving signals from the ground. Once more the siren sounded, and we knew that our first raid was over, and that the hostile machines had returned to their bases. The losses, as published in the newspaper, estimated the deaths at forty-five, and the injured at two hundred and seven.

The other evening, as I mentioned, I called on Mr. Sharp. I arrived before he had returned from the Embassy, and in the interval, I had a pleasant visit with Mrs. Sharp, the daughter and two sons. They were very cordial. Mr. Sharp did not seem to be able to do enough for me, and insisted that I call every time that I am in Paris—that the latch string will hang out for me. He said he was writing you.

The box with the cards from Ethel, Joseph and Kumano, came today, and I can assure you it was not kept waiting at the door. I was down to the last cigarette.

Hoping that you are all as well and happy as I am,

Your loving son,

William.

A. E. F., France,
February 10, 1918.

Dear Wain—

Believe me, I was mighty glad to hear from you. My letters from the States have been irregular and far between, and a little news from a good friend goes a long way.

Life here is so different from what I have been accustomed to, that I long for a word from home and friends. It has been my fortune to be one of a large family, and to associate with them and with long-time friends from childhood. Now, I am in contact with acquaintances who were strangers yesterday. New faces come and go each day. I am often lonely, and yearn for the old familiar faces. I don't like to be alone, and fortunately am very busy all the daylight hours. This occupies your mind, and you only think of what your part in the great game of war may be. I am afraid sometimes that my ambitions, even as an aviator, soar a bit too high.

Let me tell you what I have been doing since my arrival, and I think you will realise that a good deal has been accomplished. We were sent at once to an advanced training school, where we practically had to learn flying all over. In the States, we flew what is called the "Dep" control with a wheel. Here we fly a stick control—a lever instead of a wheel. You are started on a large aeroplane with a low-powered motor, and as you improve, the machines become smaller and the motors very high-powered. When you reach the stage of instruction where you have mastered the Nieuport 15 with 120 H. P.

THE FAMILY
Detroit, December 26, 1901

ed seven years, is the center of the group, standing between his grandfather and his uncle. ame from Pennsylvania to Detroit in 1836, and died in Detroit in 1903 in his eighty-

ldren—four sons and two daughters.
are his children and grandchildren:
ident of the Peoples State Bank of Detroit, his wife and nine children—four sons and

sident and General Counsel of the Michigan Central Railroad Company, his wife and
l three daughters;
lent of the Russel Wheel and Foundry Company, his wife and three children—one son

nt of the Great Lakes Engineering Works, his wife and two daughters;
hins, wife of Jere C. Hutchins, President of the Detroit United Railway Company;
ussel.
: was taken, all thirty were named Russel. Only one of the grandchildren, William's
aturity.
ons, two of the twelve granddaughters and the husbands of six others offered their

'illiam's grandfather, William K. Muir, was a prominent railroad man, and for many years
it, was General Manager of the Great Western Railway of Canada. He came from Scot-
1892, leaving a wife and six children—five daughters and one son.
ns, and the husbands of five of his eight granddaughters offered their services in the great war.

THE FAMILY

Detroit, December 26, 1901

William Muir Russel, aged seven years, is the center of the group, standing between his grandfather and his uncle.

Dr. George B. Russel came from Pennsylvania to Detroit in 1836, and died in Detroit in 1903 in his eighty-eighth year, leaving six children—four sons and two daughters.

The others in the group are his children and grandchildren:

George H. Russel, President of the Peoples State Bank of Detroit, his wife and nine children—four sons and five daughters;

Henry Russel, Vice-President and General Counsel of the Michigan Central Railroad Company, his wife and five children—two sons and three daughters;

Walter S. Russel, President of the Russel Wheel and Foundry Company, his wife and three children—one son and two daughters;

John R. Russel, President of the Great Lakes Engineering Works, his wife and two daughters;

Mrs. Sarah Russel Hutchins, wife of Jere C. Hutchins, President of the Detroit United Railway Company;

Miss Anne Davenport Russel.

At the date the picture was taken, all thirty were named Russel. Only one of the grandchildren, William's elder brother, died before maturity.

Four of the six grandsons, two of the twelve granddaughters and the husbands of six others offered their services in the great war.

On the maternal side, William's grandfather, William K. Muir was a prominent railroad man, and for many years before his removal to Detroit, was General Manager of the Great Western Railway of Canada. He came from Scotland, and died in Detroit in 1892, leaving a wife and six children—five daughters and one son.

Five of his seven grandsons, and the husbands of five of his eight granddaughters offered their services in the great war.

William was the only one who did not come home.

motor, you are ready for your acrobatics or stunt flying. Three stunts among others, which are used to great advantage in fighting, must be mastered perfectly before going further.

The first is the vertical spiral. In this, you put your machine in a position perpendicular to the earth instead of the normal parallel position, slip towards the ground in spirals and a steep slide. This sounds simple, but your machine can get into many different positions if you are not exceedingly careful. The second acrobatic is the vertical sideslip, which is of the utmost value in falling away from your pursuer, if he gains the superior position. It is peculiar that a machine will fall with greater speed off to one side than it will forwards. This is because in the vertical sideslip, in which the machine is tilted sideways to a vertical position, all air pressure of the wing surface is removed, and the machine falls free. The last and most important and difficult is the *renversement*, which is used for making a quick turn without losing any altitude.

The higher you are, the better and safer. The whole operation takes about five seconds. The machine is pulled upwards, and at the same time thrown over on its back. It is then pointed towards the ground, and brought out going in the opposite direction. It is mighty hard to explain it in words, but you may get some conception of the movements from my crude drawings. (See next page.) When you are first learning this trick, you nearly always do a loop or tail spin because of over-control. Every student, in learning, has much experience with loops and tail spins, and so they do not teach you how to do them, but how to get out of them.

After completing these acrobatics, which is ordinarily done in three days' time, you arc placed on a regular fighting machine, either a Spad 180 H. P. motor or a 15 metre Nieuport. With this, you practice what you have learned so far, and then are instructed in squadron flying, such as "V" formations, rectangular formations and the like. The days of individual fighting have just about passed away. You and your squadron now fight the German with his squadron. After you have finished your squadron formation flying, the next step is training in aerial gunnery, a course of two or three weeks' duration. It is at this point that I am now, but by the time you receive this letter, I hope to have seen some active service.

The work continues to be more and more fascinating, and in my opinion, it is the highest and most important branch of the service. These little machines, with their terrific speed of 130 miles an hour, give you sensations absolutely new to human experience. You understand that I am in chasse work, scout pursuit fighting, not bombing or observation or photographic work. I wish I had time to explain the so-called "contact" work, and how important it will be in winning battles by giving aid and diminishing the loss to the troops with which the aeronaut is in contact.

The other night, I witnessed my first air raid. It was thrilling enough for my quiet nature. The rumour that it was coming was beginning to be considered a false alarm, and almost forgotten, when the long expected siren, announcing the raid, was sounded. It was about 11:30, and ten minutes later, the German machines were over Paris. After the warning, there was the long sickening wait, and a feeling of total helplessness. No place was safe. Then, in the distance, the sharp crack of the anti-aircraft guns could be heard, followed by the low hum of the German motors. The sound became more and more distinct, then the hollow thundering of the bombs could be heard. The helpless feeling grows upon you, as you hear one bomb fall in front, then one behind, then on either side. You are sure the next will find you. As we stood on the balcony of our room, other motors could be heard flying low, and then we could see the French machines, with their little red, white and green lights, flit about, signalling to each other. Their motors have a distinctly different sound from the German motors.

After fifteen minutes of this uproar, the city was again plunged in silence, except for the sound of an occasional French plane. Only a short period elapsed, however, before the anti-aircraft guns again began their deadly work. Two machines were forced to land; one, a Frenchman who had motor trouble; the other a German, whose machine fell in flames. This lasted about a quarter of an hour, until the enemy planes returned to their bases. The invaders were evidently divided into two groups, and took the city from opposite sides at about a half an hour's interval.

The damage done to buildings was considerable, but no military advantage was accomplished. The loss of life was estimated at several hundred. It is a disgusting, dastard way of carrying on war, and unless it becomes absolutely necessary to fight fire with fire, I hope we may not be called upon to retaliate.

I have now spent quite a while in and about Paris, and evidently it is not the old Paris of which we have heard. The city is in darkness at 9:30 every evening. The women without chaperons are so numerous, and so affectionate to soldiers that one has to fight them off. If you sit down in a restaurant, they think it is their duty to teach you French and begin babbling fondly at once. On account of the novelty, I think, the American uniform is the attraction, regardless of the man in it, and the wings of the aviator seem to make it more so. The worst of it is, we now wear double wings in the place of the single one, which makes us just so much more conspicuous.

Well, Wain, I hope this is not too long and too much about myself to bore you, but I am in a world alone with unknown people, and there is little else to talk about to an old friend like yourself. At any rate these are only the beginnings of tales I hope to tell you some day.

I was mighty glad to hear that you were so much better, and hope that you will not have to sever connections with Detroit. It will not prevent me from visiting you, though, if I am spared to go back. You have picked my favourite country in the States for travel, and I hope to be knocking on your door as a guest sometime. As for the young lady, give her my best, and tell her for me how fortunate I think she is. Heartiest congratulations, and the best of luck to you.

As ever,

Bill.

To Mr. Charles Wainwright Stephens,
Albuquerque,
New Mexico, U. S. A.

A. E. F., France,
February 15, 1918.

Dear Father—

My daily routine is about the same as usual—plenty of physical work and an abundance of safety and good health. My instruction is rapidly drawing to a close. There is not the slightest cause of alarm for you, however. Many things will probably occur, and much time will pass before the crucial test comes. Outside of one or two rubs, I have known nothing but comfort. This does not include any frills like the grate fire in the library and home cooking, but I have had reminders of home in the fine boxes which have been arriving every day. Many others besides myself join in thanking you all for being good angels.

My flying, of late, has been much more regular, and I feel that I have almost acquired the art, even on these little high-powered 130-mile-an-hour machines. It is truly a pleasure to fly one. Their response to the slightest move is so quick. As one of the boys said, "If you wish to turn to the right, you merely think it, and you are headed in that direction." The days now are busily occupied. After flying for an hour or so, we attend classes in practical motor work, in learning how to correct jams of machine guns, in adjusting a compass, in leading a squadron, in drawing maps, in bombing, and last of all, in shooting with a revolver at a stationary object, with a rifle at a moving object, with a shot gun at clay pigeons, and finally, with a machine gun at balloons (toy). My favourite recreation is the squadron flying, although it is very difficult. We go off on long tours all over the country—just follow the leader through the blue and the clouds. I have not had a chance yet of leading one of these *cotillons*, but I am sure my time will come soon. Then, in all spare moments, we practice acrobatics, and repeat the stunts in the air over and over again.

The mail is now beginning to come much more on schedule, and I have received as many as five letters in one day. Two of them were from Europe, Cousin Catharine Leggat in England, and Erie Devlin in France; also a nice box of what the English officers call "sweeties" from Cousin Maud Ledyard. Anne and Helen's carefully packed box, when it reached me, contained only the remnant of a box of figs, a paper of salted peanuts, and two tins of bouillon tablets, for which I am grateful, but have not yet any great need.

I had the pleasure of dining the other evening with Major William Thaw, late of the Lafayette Esquadrille, who came to the field to inspect. We had a long talk about the Hill School, and I was able to get him to tell a few of his experiences. I am sure that I have done right in my choice. To be a chasse pilot aviator is the highest type of war service. I wish I could write you more. I know it would interest you, and feel sure that it would be consoling as well. I would like to have you feel as I do—safe and happy in the air, and only waiting to do my share.

I gather from your letters that you have suffered more from cold weather in Detroit than we, who are not actually in the trenches, have in France. For a time, it was very cold and disagreeable, but the latter half of January and so far into February, it has not been unpleasant except that always for flying the damp, misty mornings are most uncomfortable. In camp, there is no evidence of food shortage—good white bread and plenty of sugar. The roast beef, however, is not above suspicion, and on beef day, we diet to a certain extent. On the whole, our mess is very good—certainly good enough. One thing of which we never have enough is cigarettes. Remember that it is impossible to send too many. Occasionally the canteen will get a shipment, and you ought to see the rush.

It is fine to know that all of you, and there are so many, are well at home. Add me to the list. I really never felt better—out of doors all day long, and for that matter, night too, continually occupied with congenial work. Love to all.

Your loving son,

William.

A. E. F., France,
February 23, 1918.

Dear Father—

To my disappointment, I am again located where I can get no flying. It goes against the grain with me to stay on the ground all the time, and at that, shut in an office trying to fix my attention upon things far away from my thoughts. It is only because I am promised that it will be a short assignment that I am reconciled to endure it.

I helped yesterday to pack a motor of one of the Zeppelins which was brought down in France at the time Germany lost seven in a bunch after an unsuccessful raid on England. It was the L-49, and is being shipped to Washington for exhibition purposes. It is a huge motor, one of four which a zeppelin carries. I do not wonder that Germany proposes to give up this means of inhuman bombardment with the small results attained. The only reason seems to be, however, that she thinks the frightfulness is not commensurate with the expense.

I have heard that Maury has given up pilot's work, and gone into the observation end of flying, and that he is now at the front, flying as an observer for a French pilot. Ed. Buford, whom you will remember, my room-mate in Chicago, has done exceedingly well, and is now at the front flying a Spad chasse machine in the French Esquadrille. He has had four or five encounters, but has not got a Boche to his credit yet. I am sure it won't be long before he will make a record. Andy King has also left us, and is working on a Breguet in day bombing work. He is perfectly infatuated with the game, and is endeavouring to get the rest of us to give up chasse work and go with him.

It is not such a terrible strain on a man, as you are accompanied by another, who is just as much interested in watching for trouble as you are. This, too, is unquestionably the future manner of air fighting, as the time now for the sport of individual combat is over. In modern aerial warfare, your squadron takes on another squadron, and if you happen to be cut off, and are alone, then only do you have to take on another machine or another squadron by yourself. The boys with the French squadron, the old Lafayette Esquadrille men, tell me that the time for two-place machines and strict squadron flying has come. You must either keep in formation or drop out and beat it for your aerodrome. Of course, however, if you are cut off and attacked by an enemy squadron, or can tackle one or two Boches, you will fight them.

My last letter from you was dated January 28th, written from Atlantic City. The insignia and a package from Helen arrived, and papers and magazines come regularly. Aside from French newspapers, we keep up with the world news in three English papers—the New York Herald of France, the Chicago *Tribune* of France, and the American *Daily Mail*. You really get far more foreign news than we do, except, of course, what we are able to see and hear from others over here.

It is amazing to learn what a number of Americans were and are in the French and British service.

I can report perfect health as usual, a little too fat if anything for my present job. I have not been bothered with a cold since my stormy auto truck trips in December, and fortunately, my stomach now relishes army food more than the club delicacies.

With love to all.

Your loving son,

William.

A. E. F., France,
March 2, 1918.

Dear Father—

Everything is running smoothly, and I am keeping in the best of condition—a perfectly safe job; no need for anyone to worry.

Last night Angus Smith invited me to dine with Julie Russel and himself at the Hotel Petrograd. I could not go because of a previous engagement with the Sepulchres, a French family who have been very nice to me. Lieutenant Lazard, whom I met at St. Nazaire, where he had charge of the German prisoners, married one of the three Sepulchre daughters. He gave me a letter of introduction and they have been very cordial, and I have had several delightful dinners at their house—not only delightful, but humorous. None of them speaks English, and I must either speak French or silence rules the board. Their politeness is wonderful; they never smile even at my French. Two sons are in the war—one in the infantry and one in aviation.

Evening before last was spent with Ed. Buford and Lieutenant Adams, formerly of the French Flying Corps, and I have not had such an interesting time in many a day. Adams talked from four in the afternoon until eleven o'clock in the evening; not in any boastful way, but picturing conditions, and giving us advice. Once more I realised, although my training is practically completed, how little I knew. You have got to be there to know. We will probably start at the front in French squadrons, two of us amateurs flying with sixteen experienced pilots in formation, where we will be able to witness the combats and hear and see the shrapnel bursting about us. In this way, we will accustom ourselves to actual air-war conditions, and at the same time, be nursed and protected by experienced aviators. This will probably continue for two months.

An interesting thing he told me was that one evening he was turned over, bottom side up, five times from the concussion of large shells; another that you are a great deal safer twenty miles behind the German lines than directly over the front. Another thing, which seemed contrary to what I had heard, was that it will be impossible to do away with the little machines, one seaters or monoplanes, because they are necessary to protect the large machines. If we had large machines only, and not a sufficient number of scout planes to protect them, the Germans, with their small fast machines, would play havoc with our craft.

The first of the Liberty motors have been received. I was fortunate enough to have a look at them but have not yet seen one running. There are great tales concerning what they can actually do. I am so proud of them, and glad to see something so great from home, that I feel like taking the liberty of hugging one.

I met Washie Patterson from Ann Arbor the other night, when I was dining with my friend, Lieutenant Reilly, now a Captain, who has been so kind to me at St. Nazaire and Paris. Washie was at the Hill, and is now enlisted in the French Artillery, stationed at Fontainbleau. I have run across Billy McKim, too. He is also a Hill boy, and is a private in the Medical Corps, working on a new form of gas. Speaking of gas; the new German stuff is terrible to cope with. It is an invention of the devil, and not only destroys your eyes, throat and lungs, but will penetrate your clothes, and burns into the body wherever it is moist.

The newspapers today are far from encouraging—Russia's flat demoralization and Rumania's rumoured peace terms. That poor little country has suffered so fearfully, and is so unprotected that one cannot help but think that it has some reason to hunt cover; but will they find it?

Yesterday, a letter came from Colonel Hutton, enclosing a communication from Colonel Littebrant to General Pershing, inquiring for the whereabouts of the Honourable Henry Russel's son, and his correct address. Reply was made in true military form, and through the proper army channels. You have, no doubt, heard from me in the meantime. The system is much improved, and your mail now comes more regularly. Your last box with the Deities and Omars was truly a benefaction. Cigarettes, as usual, are few and far between.

Well, father, to my great disappointment I am again for a time away from flying, only waiting for further orders. My next assignment is as much a mystery to me as to you. Am in the best of health. With love to all.

Your loving son,

William.

A. E. F., France,
March 12, 1918.

Dear Father—

I am still stationed in a quiet place. The only dangerous instrument near at hand is a typewriter, and the only disturbing action is that the welcome spring breezes muss the paper.

I have had a ripple of pleasant excitement today. Colonel Hutton writes that orders for me are *en route*. It looks as if my days of leisure are rapidly drawing to a close. It has been a quiet rest, and I am in the pink of health and condition, except a little too plump, A couple of weeks' good work-out in the real service for which I am pining, and I will soon reduce myself to normal.

I was shocked to read this morning that Wallie Winters, one of the boys whom I have got to know best, was killed yesterday in a fight with four Boche machines. Just a week ago, he was credited with bringing down his first adversary, a two-seated Gotha, which I can assure you is something of a feat. He is only twenty-two years old. Only two weeks ago, Wallie and Andy King and I spent a pleasant evening together at the Hotel Crillon. He was bold and brave, even to rashness, and as he told us of his high ambitions and what he expected to accomplish, I feared that without a little more prudence, his time would soon come.

Last Friday night, I experienced my third air raid. The second was more of a scare than anything else, but the third was the real thing, although the damage done was not as severe as the first. I think this was due to the fact that the French were much better prepared this time. The anti-aircraft barrage was much more accurate and strong. We saw, once more, an enemy's machine fall in flames in the city. When the warning sounded. Captain Reilly, Lieutenant Gulliver and I were calling at the Sepulchres, and although they were thoughtful of others, one could not imagine a more terrified family. The doorbell rang a thousand times, and people from the street, especially women and little children, were taken in and allowed to go down into the cellar.

We, who were in the house, took shelter in a room on the second floor, and all the lights were turned out. Then the family, distracted with terror, turned to me for salvation, and on their knees with prayerful pleas, asked why I did not do something. We waited patiently for about twenty minutes for the Gothas to arrive, but nothing could be heard except the screeching sirens and the low roar of the French motors patrolling the city, while here and there you could distinguish their coloured lights. For a moment, relief came with the thought that it was merely another alarm, but before I could suggest it, the crack of the aircraft guns began. A few minutes later, the low hollow roar of the bombs was heard. The raid came in three waves, and lasted nearly three hours. The family and the people who had gathered in the house were restored to a state of quiet and self-control before we left. None was injured, and we were unable to learn much about the loss elsewhere until Sunday morning—about thirty killed and fifty wounded.

I could not help but think how fortunate, if one can say that, it is that the Boches have chosen to raid London so much and not Paris. I am sure the French, with all their amazing bravery and endurance, could not bear to be under continued and repeated attacks of this kind. They are too high-strung. They are, however, preparing against numerous raids on Paris. All the valuable statuary and buildings are being carefully sandbagged and boarded up. The Arc de Triomphe is practically covered, likewise Napoleon's Column.

Sunday, we confiscated one of Uncle Sam's automobiles, and started out on a very educational, as well as interesting trip through Versailles and Villa Coubley. At Versailles, we collided quite through accident, and I assure you it was an accident, with two venerable Y. M. C. A. ladies, who took it upon themselves that we should not leave Versailles without seeing the sights. Helpless as lambs, we were collared and led about through streets and galleries and palaces. If you want to know anything about Versailles, we can furnish the information. Thanks to our elderly friends, I can vouch for the group that nothing was overlooked.

Later: The siren, giving the warning of another raid, has just sounded. The lights will be extinguished at any moment. I will delay my letter until quiet comes.

Everything is now over, and, thank God, all of my friends, as far as I can learn, are safe and sound as before. However, I am afraid that it will prove to be the worst raid yet.

They are thrilling to watch and you boil with rage at your helplessness and such despicable and useless cruelty.

But to conclude my story of Versailles: After we had seen everything possible and heard it described in detail, we were able to beat a polite but masterly retreat from our instructive friends and get to our car, with loss only of time. I then took it upon myself to lead the squadron. None of the party had ever been near an aeroplane so I took them to Villa Coubley. The machines were landing and taking off directly in front of us, so that the party could see their entire mechanism and action. They seemed to be appalled at the smallness of some of the planes, and the bigness of others. One machine, the largest in the world, was there with a wing spread of one hundred and sixty-five feet. I was proud to be able to introduce the party to some of my fine friends at the field, and after that we drove around and made a close inspection of the damage done by the air raid.

An automobile ride on a beautiful spring day, with such remarkable and interesting incidents, would be the event of a lifetime to many people.

Love to all. Well.

Your loving son,

William.

Aviation Section,
American Expeditionary Forces,
Via New York.

Dear Father—

Thanks to our mutual friend, Colonel Hutton, I am again stationed at an aviation camp, where I am able to get all the flying that one desires, the only hindrance being bad weather. Last Friday evening I promised to have dinner with Julie Russel, but owing to a terrible explosion in one of the munition dumps in the neighbourhood

Aviation Section
American Expeditionary Forces
Via New York.

Dear Father,

Thanks to our mutual friend Col. Hutton, I am again stationed at an aviation camp where I am able to get all the flying that one desires, the only hindrance being bad weather. Last Friday evening, I promised to have dinner with Julie Russel but owing to a terrible explosion in one of the munition dumps in the neighborhood of Paris, I was unable to meet her. At the time, I had some three hundred and fifty troops at my disposal together with ten trucks, when word came from Capt. Reilly to rush all to the scene of the accident to place them at the services of the French authorities. This I did and I can assure you, we were among the first to arrive at the scene. Everywhere within a circuit of three miles, men, women, and children could be seen running about hysterically with bad face and scalp wounds, the result of broken glass. The Red Cross and Y.M.C.A. workers handled all these cases and we rushed ahead to the scene of the explosion. It was still very active and in fact remained so for

MSS. OF FIRST PAGE OF LETTER OF MARCH 20, 1918

of Paris I was unable to meet her.

At the time I had some three hundred and fifty troops at my disposal, together with ten trucks, when word came from Captain Reilly to rush all to the scene of the accident and to place them at the services of the French authorities. This I did, and I can assure you we were among the first to arrive at the scene. Everywhere within a circuit of three miles, men, women and children could be seen running about hysterically with bad face and scalp wounds, the result of broken glass.

The Red Cross and Y. M. C. A. workers handled all these cases and we rushed ahead to the scene of the explosion. It was still very active, and, in fact, remained so for a day and a half. Several factories about the dump were totally destroyed, and it was in these that our men concentrated their work. Many dead bodies were recovered, and we were able to take out a few living people who had been badly crushed and we hurried them to the American Hospital in our trucks. The work, I assure you, was far from pleasant, and lasted from two o'clock in the afternoon until midnight, when we all marched home. At camp, Captain Reilly commended the men highly for their work and gave them the next morning off. It was the Americans who handled practically the entire situation, and I think it was a far greater calamity than the press has made known.

The same night on returning, Lieutenant Ormsby, who had been left in command of the post in my absence, informed me that my orders had come to proceed to another instruction centre, and that they were awaiting me at headquarters. Needless to say, I was the happiest man in the world.

The next morning, I went into Paris, received my orders, made the necessary purchases and met Julie at the Hotel Petrograd for luncheon. We had a pleasant chat together, which was terminated very suddenly just as I was kissing her goodbye when special orders came to me to report at once. At dinner that night I was most pleasantly surprised on being presented with a beautiful gold watch and testimonial by Captain Reilly; it was a present from the officers and every enlisted man in the post. I was absolutely dumbfounded. It was all so unnecessary and so unexpected and undeserved, and of course I made a bungle of my speech.

I bade farewell to everyone that night and left early the next morning for the place where I now am, thanks be unto heaven.

I found here many of the boys whom I came over with and have had a great reunion. Among them are Sandy Weathered (of Detroit),

Harry Colburn, Bill Hoeveler, Andy King, Rowland Potter (formerly of Detroit), Jeff Blanchard, and Vanderhoef. Why we are all here I do not know, but think it is probably a concentration camp where we may all keep our hands in the flying game until the time shall come when our machines are ready. I still have my Spad, that is the plane assigned to my exclusive use, and I am up in it as often as I can.

I had a long talk with Rowly Potter last night. I had not seen him since school days, when our Hill football team played with the Hotch-kiss team, of which Rowly was a member.

I was very sorry to hear that my dear friend, Andy Ortmayer, was killed last week in England. We thought he was the best flyer at Rantoul. You remember him, I think. You met him at the hotel and brought him down to the boat just before we sailed last October. I have heard no details of the accident, but it is authentic as it comes from George Fisher, his closest friend. Captain Miller, another of the boys whom I liked very much, was killed at the front on the same day. He was with Ed. Buford's squadron. But, father, this is enough of this kind of news.

I am very pleased where I am now, although as usual the luxuries of home are lacking. The quarters are poor, but we have beds, at least double-deckers with chicken wire to sustain the thin mattresses, and a warm room to go to bed in. The morning, however, is too unpleasant to speak of, but there is always plenty of cold, cold water to wash with, and that is a refresher.

Now, for the brighter side. The mess is excellent, and the American Red Cross have a wonderful building with a good restaurant and real American girls waiting on the table; they are doing splendid work, and everyone pays them the utmost respect. They have actually enabled the Y. M. C. A. to close their doors at this post. Then, as for the men who are stationed here, a great number of them I am happy to call my friends; they are wonders, certainly a picked bunch of men, many of them college fellows. We have abundant liberty, practically being our own bosses, but we try to uphold the prestige of the camp at all times.

Yesterday we were carefully inspected by General Pershing, himself, and I think he was quite pleased with the post. A wonderful exhibition of flying was given, including aerial combats, acrobacy, squadron flying and a general review. Estes Armstrong, who was with us in New York, had a bad fall during the exhibition and for a time all hope of his recovery was given up. Today, however, he is doing better, and they think he will come through all right except for the loss or stiffening of one leg. He is one of the best fellows in the camp.

Well, father, this about completes the news for this issue, and the next will follow very soon, I hope. There is a great deal of interest and of happenings where I now am. I hope that you, at home, are all well and happy. There is no need of sympathy for me; I am in the best of health with many wonderful men around me. Love to all.

Your loving son,

William

March 20, 1918.

A. E. F., France,
March 27th, 1918.

Dear Father—

I am no longer associated with typewriters, but am at one of the flying fields where flying is abundant—a little too much, if anything—six and seven hours every day with the exception of Sundays and days of bad weather. I am still using a chasse machine 120 H. P. Nieuport, but dare not claim yet that I will be allowed to follow up this work and become a *Chasse* Pilot.

Another branch which would not be very objectionable if I do not make good as a scout is day bombing. In the latter, you have a larger machine carrying an extra person with an extra gun. I hope that I will not have to follow artillery observation or contact patrol. The work does not seem so attractive or exciting to me. I suppose when one's heart is set on a thing, any other alternative does not seem agreeable Maury Hill has chosen artillery observation; Ed. Buford, chasse; and Andy King, day bombing.

The air was full of wild rumours last week in Paris, and everyone seemed to be nervous and ill at ease on account of the imminence of the Big Offensive. I left Paris in the midst of the preparations, and just before the big gun began its deadly work. Some of the boys who were in Paris getting their planes told me that for a few hours utter confusion reigned. No one could determine that the source of such explosives was a long range gun. It was a beautifully clear day, and no planes could be seen in the air. At first, it was thought that a new machine had been invented which could climb to previously unknown heights. After two or three hours, the community settled down to a semblance of quiet and order. Gendarmes went about the streets beating drums both to warn and distract the people. Right after this came another air raid, and finally the Big Offensive almost at the doors of Paris. It is no wonder that the city was for a short time almost overwhelmed with terror. To many of the people, the first thought was flight from Paris. This caused great congestion at the railroad stations. It was not long, however, they tell me, before order was restored and the courage of the French reasserted itself.

Rumour kept our flying camp in a state of mind as well. We heard that all finished pilots would go at once to the defence of Paris; also that many of our divisions would immediately become reserves to the British and French Aviation Forces. This is only part of the news which kept us guessing, and you can imagine the life we have lived.

I found here practically all of my old friends, and also a great many new men from Cornell, and last but not least, Rowly Potter. He has been ordered here, but has done no flying yet. Another acquaintance whom I found is Doctor Goldthwaite. I went to see him the other day about my stomach which has been kicking up a wee bit. It bothered me a good deal and seemed to throw my eyes out of kilter.

I have to report my first accident—nothing serious, however. I was working with Quentin Roosevelt. There was a very high wind, and I was rolled over on my back on the ground, wrecking the machine badly. I did not even have as much as a bruise; was merely pushed out in the mud and soiled my clothes. Quentin Roosevelt is now in charge of us. He is an awfully nice fellow and a beautiful flyer. If I am not mistaken, he is also going to take up chasse work.

Our next accomplishment will be night flying. They have just established it, and I will commence my work next week, and think it will be quite thrilling.

Well, father, there is little more to say which one can tell, but I can assure you that I am quite well. Am getting even more flying than I wished. I never thought this time would come. Two two-hour flights in the morning, and two two-hour flights in the afternoon at about a sixteen-thousand-foot altitude. We usually cut off about fifteen minutes on each formation; five machines to a formation.

Your loving son,

William.

A. E. F., France,
April 1, 1918.

Dear Helen—

Nothing but blinding rain and strong westerly winds for four days, which have afforded us a much-needed rest.

For the two weeks preceding, we were worked to the limit, and kept continually under a nervous strain, which, at times, is very trying. As long as the weather permitted, and for a while it was beautiful, we were at it from seven in the morning until seven and seven-thirty in the evening; darkness only ending the day's work of eight hours of flying, fifty rounds of wing shooting, and practice with machine guns on the range. It was pleasant work, but, as I said, is most trying because of the nervous strain.

In my letter of some time ago, I described the acrobatics which are compulsory for each chasse pilot to take. Our machines have been strengthened to stand the extra strain. All of the sensations are pleasant except the side-slip, where you fall off to one side perpendicularly. This is the worst I have yet encountered, and you may be sure that one does it only when he is ordered to. You are actually torn away from your seat, and your life belt is all that holds you in the machine. At the same time, your stomach rests in your mouth. You can probably understand why the rain is such a friend in need after you have worked for a week endeavouring to perfect such stunts.

After satisfying certain French *moniteurs* that these manoeuvres have been mastered, we were assigned to another field to perfect our squadron flying. This is most interesting work, but a little tedious, as you have to do almost too much flying. You stand formation as usual at seven o'clock, and then have to go on four different flights of two hours each before sunset. This flying all takes place above an altitude of sixteen thousand feet. You fly generally in a formation of five machines, with only a small space between them. The formations are all of different types. The most common is the inverted V, like a flock of wild geese. You fly all over France, seldom covering the same ground twice. If your motor cuts out, you land at the most convenient place practicable. You are often left a long time in such a position, as it takes two men to start one of these high-powered machines. The little machines, though, are fascinating, and you soon commence to baby the one assigned to you like a pet dog.

My work continues under the guidance of Lieutenant Quentin Roosevelt, who is a wonderful flyer and a good instructor, although, as he admits, he was indirectly responsible for my first mishap, which, however, hurt nothing but my uniform and the machine. The first day of this bad weather, he sent us out to try the air and test some machines. A young fellow named Warwick took one. Rich another, and I the third. The machines were parked in a line along the front and in the lee of the hangars. My motor was started first, and I commenced taxiing out to take off against the wind from the hangars.

After going about fifty feet, the wind got under my tail, and spun me around and tipped me over. I was underneath, but my dignity only was crushed, and I crawled out in the mud from beneath the machine, with many worried eyes scanning me. They insisted that I was hurt, and I insisted that I was not. I looked to see what the other machines were doing, and to my surprise, found that they had collided head on into each other. The wind had also played havoc with them, sending them into each other's arms. With three perfectly good machines wrecked in one minute, and no one to blame except the wind, Quentin decided to call off flying. He has something of his father in him, and is willing to take chances.

This kind of weather has continued since and one can only talk about flying. This form of aviation is commonly called "barracks flying," and is absolutely tabooed. When off the field all flying ceases.

Yesterday being Easter Sunday, and a disagreeable day, my thoughts wandered along serious lines and carried me back home. I do not like to be pessimistic. I think I will come home all right, but I do not see a chance of returning for a long while.

While I was at the Y. M. C. A. getting some hot chocolate and sympathy, I read in the *Stars and Stripes* that Ithaca was going dry in October. The man behind the counter asked me if it was because I was a Cornell man that I was interested. He said he was there in the class of 1907. We talked on for a few moments so as to size each other up, and I rather took to him, and asked him if he knew Pat Wardwell. That was enough introduction for him. He told me to be sure and tell Pat that I had shaken the hand of Bill Forbes of Cleveland. He invited me into his room, and we talked over old times and friends at Cornell. I found the welcome company and sympathy for which I had been praying.

We were given a twenty-three hour leave over Sunday, which very foolishly, I did not use. Some of the boys went to Orleans and attended services at the Eglise St. Croix. They said the singing was beautiful and the sermon most impressive. I was sorry I did not go. It would have taken me out of the rut into which one so naturally falls in camp.

Love to all. Well.

Your loving brother,

Bill.

To Mrs. H. F. Wardwell,
Grosse Pointe Park, Mich.

Dear Eleanor—

The last two weeks have brought with them nothing but westerly winds, drizzling rains, and low-hanging clouds, which have made flying almost impossible. However, if this may be of any advantage to our Allies at the front in the great offensive, we, in our safer positions, cannot complain. Quentin Roosevelt, now in charge of us, has pushed us to get every hour's flying possible, and in some instances, he took rather big chances.

I had an interesting experience the other day. The clouds were exceedingly low, but looked broken up, so we were sent out in a formation of eight machines to fly above the clouds. We formed to the right of the field in the usual way, and then started out across country. It was perfectly beautiful. The clouds, with the sun shining on them from above, looked like silvery fleece. All went fine until the leader had to make a forced landing because of engine trouble. As is the rule, the machine directly following, which happened to be mine, has to descend with him to near the ground to make sure no injury comes to him in landing. All was O. K.

He went down safely; and then I turned to rejoin the squadron. I passed through the first bank of clouds, and could not find it; then through the second, and saw nothing. I then figured out my direction as well as I could, and dropped down through the clouds to return to the field. Nothing looked familiar, and I wandered aimlessly about at a low altitude below the clouds looking for some landmark. My gasoline was just about out. I knew I must soon land, when I saw a town. I made for it, chose my field, and landed.

After much French babbling, I located myself in the town of Selles sur Cher, some seventy kilometres away from home. I found there one of our divisions stationed temporarily, and their C. O's were very courteous. They gave me luncheon and fifty litres of gasoline. Their intentions were the best, I know, but the gas which they gave me was diluted a bit too much, and burned poorly. It carried me to the town of Gevres, where I located an aviation field. They drained the gasoline system, and again filled me, and I started on my way. Fate, however, was against me. My machine refused to return, and on using the second full tank of essence, I dropped into another little French town. They informed me it was Vineul, and that there was a French aviation school on the outskirts of the city. I rose, circled the city, and dropped into the aerodrome.

It was amusing to me to see the machines they were flying—the early types of Farmans and Caudrons; big bulky machines, with an approximate speed of about fifty miles an hour. But why criticize my hosts? They were very kind, and gave me gas and advice as to how to return. Their directions were very vague, or I was stupid, because for the third time, I descended, out of gas, in a town I knew well—Chateauroux. It was an easy flight from here, and I landed at the field at six o'clock in the evening, having left it at seven in the morning. One way to see France. When I reported to Quentin Roosevelt, he greeted me cordially, but all he said was, "Am glad you brought the machine back safely."

For the other, and less successful experience: I left at the same time in the morning to partake in a cross-country flight. On reaching the River Cher, we took our course in a northwesterly direction along the river. In the worst of all imaginable places, my motor stopped dead. I had good altitude, so it gave me time to choose my field. I felt trouble long before it came, but headed down right into what looked to be a field surrounded by a hedge. On coming closer and closer, my heart sank. My field, although the ground was good, was terribly small, and what I took to be a hedge was high poplar trees. It was too late to change, so I determined to just clear the trees on one side in order not to roll into those on the other side.

My plan was good, but the piloting poor, and in trying to clear the trees, one wing, the right upper, struck a branch of the tree next, tearing off the wing. With this supporting surface removed, my right side headed groundward, but acting so quickly I over-controlled, throwing the machine into a wing-slip on the other side, and crashed to the ground. For a minute or two, I did not move, the belt only holding me in, as the machine was balanced on her nose. Then I realised I was not hurt, undipped the belt and fell to the ground. By this time, a few of the French neighbours had congregated, and I had a difficult time explaining that I was not hurt. It was really very fortunate that I was not, but truly, I did not have a scratch. If it had not been for a stiff back, I would not have known that I fell.

The most interesting part followed. I sent a little French fellow to Chabris to telephone for the "trouble shooters" while I rested peacefully on the floor in front of a peasant's hearth. It was baking day, and the entire family took part in the operation. They wrapped the dough in burlaps and put it down on the ground near the oven. The firing of the oven was a curious procedure. They would place little bundles of sticks in it, ignite them, then clean it out, and do the same thing over and over. After an hour of this, they removed the ashes and took out a large paddle, shaped like a shovel, on which they placed the dough. This, they put in various parts of the oven, and allowed it to remain for an hour and a half. It was then removed, brushed off with a dry broom, and placed on a rack in the wall.

At seven o'clock, my camion arrived. We loaded the wreck on it and started for the field. About this time, it began raining very hard, and we spent the night in a little French town through which we were passing. I arrived at camp at noon the next day.

There has been little diversion at the field except for some entertainments during the bad weather. Most of the time is spent reading or writing.

Please tell Father I would rather have him keep my letters and not let them be published. It always looks as if a fellow was pushing himself upon the public and I do not like it. My work may be for the public but my letters are for you and him and the family.

Love to all.

Affectionately,

Bill,

To Mrs. Henry Russel, Detroit.

A. E. F., France,
April 10, 1918.

Dear Father—

The bad weather continues, no rain, but low-hanging clouds which make flying practically impossible except for the *tour de piste* where one circles the field and makes landings only. Having passed this stage of the game, my occupation consists of gathering about the fire with the rest of the warmth seekers. It is an exceedingly poor coal fire in the centre of the barracks, circumscribed with trunks on which the would-be flyers sit. If anyone should make the grave mistake of talking flying, a stick or poker is placed in his hands and the chorus sings, "*Show us how you would do it, Mr. Bones.*" Barracks flying is not encouraged.

Our time has been spent in reading and shooting. Every day, we shoot fifty rounds at clay pigeons with shot guns, thirty rounds at a target with a machine gun, and twenty-five rounds with an automatic. This routine is broken only by meals and a sojourn to the Y. M. C. A.

a branch of the tree-next, tearing off the wing. With this supporting surface removed, my right side headed ground-word, but acting as quickly I over-controlled throwing the machine into a wing slip on the other side and crashed to the ground. For a minute or two I did not move, the belt only holding me in, as the machine was balanced on her nose. Then I realized I was not hurt, un-clipped the belt and fell to the ground. By this time, a few of the french neighbors had congregated and I had a difficult time explaining that I was not hurt. It was really very fortunate and very lucky that I was not, but I truly did not have a scratch. If it had not been for a little of stiff back, I would not have known that I fell. But the most interesting part of all followed. I sent a little french fellow to Chalâis

MSS. OF PAGE OF LETTER OF APRIL 8, 1918

at 5:30 for a cup of hot chocolate and three hard biscuits. After flying, chocolate is fine. Pat's friend, Mr. Forbes, is at present the "pourer." He is a very nice fellow. This and a movie once a week are our recreations, so you see that I am not falling by the wayside in my army career in France.

Yesterday was a fine day for me in the mail. I received five letters; one from Mr. Deming Jarves from Val Fleuri, one from Wain at Albuquerque, New Mexico, informing me that he was practically well, and expected to return to Detroit to live permanently. Then, there was a letter from you and one from Eleanor, post marked Atlantic City, and one from Christine. Added to all this was a box from Cousin Catharine Leggat, bringing oranges and ginger bread right here to camp. The letters come like manna from heaven.

After two weeks in barracks, with little to keep you busy, one's thoughts are constantly inclined to be wandering back home.

Love to all.

Your loving son,

William.

A. E. F., France,
April 15, 1918.

Dear Father—

Your letter, written from the Detroit Club March 6th, came and brought a little sunshine with it.

The weather has been terrible, and my surroundings are far from pleasant, which made conditions even worse. Our only purpose in being here, however, is well attended to, and we are flying every minute possible, between storms and during showers. It has been tedious work. Some of our flights continue as long as eight hours a day with only a short break for luncheon. The other day, when I was making my altitude test in the 15-120s in which I flew at an altitude of twenty-one thousand feet, I froze two of the fingers on my left hand. The least touch of cold affects them. The doctor told me there is nothing to do except to soak them in warm water and massage frequently.

With my left hand, I work the small gas and air *manettes* which I cannot adjust with a glove or mitten on. I can keep my right hand well covered and warm. It was necessary to remain at this altitude for fifteen minutes, and when I descended, I was absolutely lost, so I dropped into the first town which I passed over, and learned from the people who immediately rushed up that I was one hundred and twenty kilometres from my proper destination. My gasoline was very low, and I knew it would be impossible to reach the field, so I decided to make a dive for the home grounds and get as near as possible. The crowd of people who had gathered about gave me general directions, and I started; but very soon the expected spitting began, and the motor stopped.

A small town was directly opposite so I spiralled down into a nearby field and again asked where I was. This proved to be a small town, only twenty-six kilometres away, a matter of only a few minutes but where was gasoline to be obtained? I wandered into the village, which, by the way, was the town where Jean d'Arc met Charles VII. Here I ran across an American military policeman, who told me that there was a camp two miles away. I telephoned, and they gave me fifty litres of gasoline. I filled the machine and endeavoured to start, but unfortunately, truck gasoline will not drive an aeroplane. As it was getting dark, I had a guard posted over the machine, and spent the night in the town.

In the early morning, I was awakened by the *femme de chambre* who asked me if I was the aviator for whom a motor was waiting. The mechanics had arrived with good essence. We drained out the poor gas, filled the machine, turned her over, and away I went, reaching the field O. K. at eleven o'clock a. m., and reported to Quentin Roosevelt. I had been gone since seven o'clock of the morning before, and this time Quentin said he was glad to see me as well as the machine safely back.

The last few days have been spent in lectures during the rain, and actual work-out the minute it ceased. Most of the acrobatics are good fun, and exceedingly pretty to watch from the ground.

Thursday, I expect to make another move, which, although not very far away, is enough south so that the weather will be more enjoyable. There, we will have a complete course in aerial combat work. One machine is sent out to patrol a certain section, and later another machine is sent up to attack it. You have all the thrills of actual warfare with its quick manoeuvres, only gun cameras replace the machine gun. Then, too, you take up toy balloons, throw them over and dive at them, shooting with the real thing. You also dive and fire at a kite, which is towed at a good length behind another machine. This camp is purely for practice in aerial gunnery. It is situated near the ocean, and is located only twelve miles from a popular summer resort. I go there with a squadron of seventeen. They are all nice fellows. We have had our advanced training together. They are all men whom I have met since my arrival in France. Three of them are from Cornell, two from Harvard, one from Princeton, one from Williams, and one from Pennsylvania.

You asked me in one of your letters whether I took part in the big show for Secretary Baker, and I have the pleasure of informing you that the privilege was mine. I flew in one of the formations over the main camp. It was at this celebration that Estes Armstrong, one of my friends in Memphis, fell and was very badly hurt. One leg was broken in several places. I am afraid it will prevent him from flying any more. He was doing acrobatics too near the ground, a very pretty but dangerous thing.

I hope Anne's troubles and the sickness in her house have passed. Her fine box with cigarettes and other things is here.

Love to all. Well.

> Your loving son,
>
> William

Third Aviation Instruction Centre,
A. E. F., France,
April 16, 1918.

Dear Father—

Just a line before flitting south for a ten days' course in aerial combat work.

I expect to leave tonight, and understand from the other boys that the new location is a very beautiful spot. The camp is on the shore of a large lake on which the various combat work and aerial gunnery are carried on. Ten miles away from the field is one of the most attractive French watering places, just now at the height of its season. If the weather is bad, we will have a chance to enjoy it; if not, I am told we will be worked from early morning until dark. At the end of this course, I am going to try for a leave. It will be my first permission. In fact, if I do get it, it will be the only leave of absence, except for an occasional weekend at the American camps, since I enlisted.

I have just got a report from Tours that Bob Townes, who is instructing there, had a bad fall yesterday. He escaped without injury, but his pupil was killed. He has not yet had any Nieuport training, and went directly into Caudron flying—a big, heavy, bulky machine. They are used for preliminary training so that a student may familiarize himself with the feeling of the air. It corresponds to the training

191

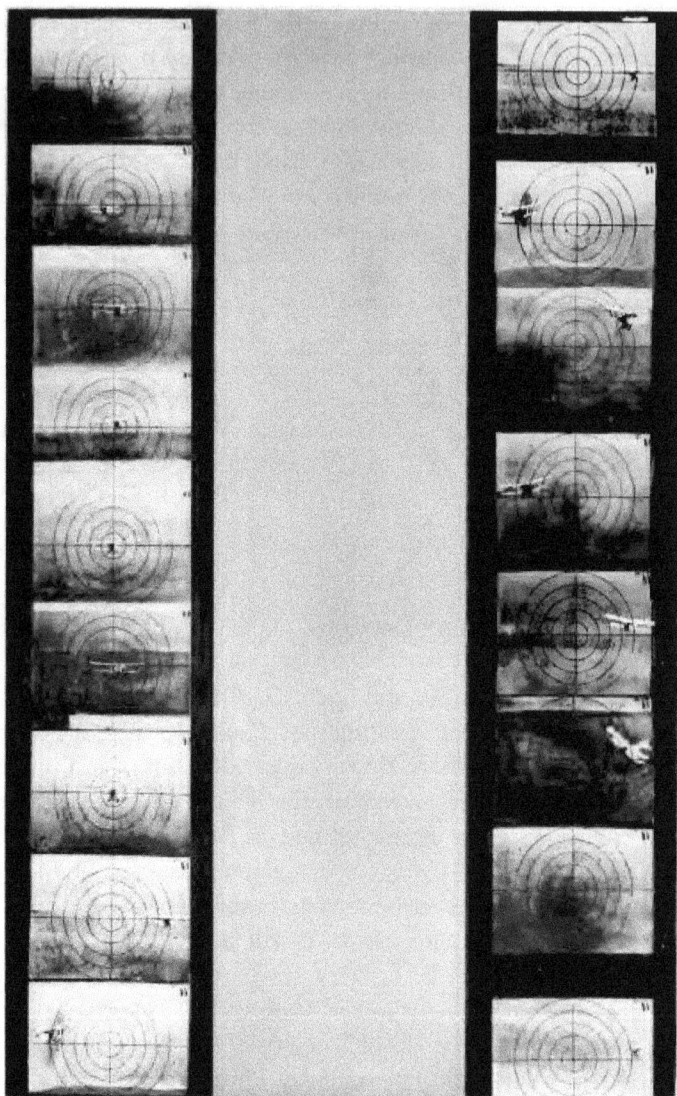

TARGET RECORD OF GUN CAMERA. SNAPSHOTS TAKEN BY
PULLING TRIGGER, THE SAME AS IF GUN WAS IN ACTUAL USE.
THE ENEMY PLANE IS SHOWN WITHIN THE TARGETS.

we had in the States.

I had a long letter from Maury Hill yesterday. He, as I wrote you, has transferred into artillery observation. He says that his machine is a very strong aeroplane, but rather heavy and awkward. He is at the front doing observation work over our own lines, not yet flying over the enemy's lines. His letter, like some of mine, is not very clear, owing to the censorship.

The boys preceding me in chasse work, we are informed, are doing very well, and at the rate they are going will soon be aces. It is gratifying, because everybody has eyes on them, and it inspires us all with pride in our work and the hope soon to get into the thick of things.

Bill Hoeveler and Vanderhoef left the other day to take up work in day bombing, a branch rapidly coming into favour. It will undoubtedly play an important part, but I am still confident that chasse work is the highest and most useful type of the service. The boys with whom I am going south are fine fellows like the rest of the aviators, but are new friends that I have made. You do not know any of them.

I wish my trip tonight were over. Railroad travel at night in France, as I have learned by experience, is done standing or sitting up. But it will be a matter of only twelve hours, and then delightful spring weather instead of rain and cold. Will write you all about it. Well.

Your loving son,

William.

Nouveau Grand Hotel,
Arcachon, (Cote d' Argent), France,
April 18, 1918.

Dear Father—

After an uncomfortable trip, I have come here to find the most charming place I have yet visited in France. Arcachon is the heaven in France for children, and apparently for the mothers and nurses who accompany them. I gather from the lovely villas scattered about, and the hotel, that it is a very fashionable place. It is the first time for a long while that I have seen dinner clothes in evidence. The recent raids on Paris, the storming of the big gun, and the beginning of the great offensive have all contributed to sending crowds here. Arcachon is on the shore, and our room looks out upon the ocean. The beautiful big casino just a few doors away is now a hospital. Dotting the beach for some three miles are little villas, peculiar structures, painted in bright colours. Behind the string of cottages, there is a bluff, having a small mountain effect, heavily grown with pines. This forms a screen for the other part of the city, which is a winter resort.

Yesterday, we drove in and out among the trees, through winding roads and charming scenery. Dick Este says it resembles Bermuda.

Last night I reported at the camp, a French school, and they told me to stay where I was, and that I need not report again until Saturday. It was certainly a message of good tidings. I have by no means lost interest, but it will be a relief for a few days to see, smell and talk about things other than aeroplanes, and a fellow without work or care ought to enjoy a three days' rest here in a comfortable hotel at this attractive resort.

On the completion of my course at the school, if I get permission, my first one and long overdue, I will either spend it here or go to Nice. After that, I will probably be assigned to a French Esquadrille where I will be fortunate enough to have a Spad and not a Nieuport plane. There is not a great deal of difference, but it seems to me that the latter is not so strong or dependable.

On the way here we had to stop off for several hours at Bordeaux and I had a good chance to see the city. Just now, and further away from the front, it seems more attractive than Paris, but of course none of the cities is in a normal condition.

I am looking forward with pleasure to the change to a summer uniform. It has been so frightfully raw and cold, especially in the heights to which I have been accustomed, that we have had to dress like polar explorers.

I wrote you about freezing my fingers, over which I have been lamenting until yesterday, when I met a boy who had frozen his nose and cheeks. He was such a shocking sight that I think I was lucky. There is no feeling yet in one finger, and the end has puffed up and become callous. I have to give it careful massage treatment frequently every day.

From my window I can see the other boys sailing on the bay, but after my night's travel with two changes, one at twelve and one at three o'clock, I am disposed to remain in this comfortable room and spend the time writing and resting.

They have done things to the railways here as well as at home. Under war time government regulations, not only have the sleeping cars been taken off so that one must sit up or often stand up, but they do not heat the cars, and towards midnight it becomes freezing cold. Luckily one can forget all this in a few hours, and I am now in satisfaction and content.

Your loving son,

William.

A. E. F., France,
May 1, 1918.

Dear Father—

When I realise that the first of May has come again and the season at Fontinalis is open once more without my being there to whip the stream, I begin to think that I have signed up for a life job at war. I had never missed a visit to that lovely stream in a single season of my life until I enlisted. Mother took me there first in swaddling clothes before I was a year old. You remember the picture.

The service and my experience in the camps at home and over here have all been extremely interesting, and I would not willingly forego them, but oh! for a couple of weeks at Fontinalis. We have all been discussing where we will spend our permissions, and I recalled many of the good times you gave me there, and was surprised to find that nearly every one of the boys would choose just such a place for a loaf if he could. It seems to us to be as far away from military discipline and mechanical work and flying as any place can be.

But the choice has been made for us by General Pershing, who has issued orders that all leaves be suspended until after the Great Offensive. All transportation facilities must be used for the armies. It is some recompense, however, for disappointment, to be at this beautiful place. It seems a shame though, that one has to work so hard and do everything to fit one's self to fight, with all the beautiful scenery, golf courses, tennis courts, yachting, swimming, fishing, etc., going to waste about us.

We have to report on the field in flying clothes at seven-thirty, and keep practicing and flying until eleven-thirty, when there is nearly a three-hour stop for lunch in accordance with the good old French custom. You understand that this is the finishing school for *chasse* pilots. At two-thirty, we report at the field again, and flying continues until eight o'clock. The rest of the time is free. At Issoudun, when it rained, we rested. Here, when the weather is inclement, we attend lectures on machine guns, deflections, jams of guns, etc. I forgot, however, to mention that we only fly until noon on Sunday, giving us a rest of a whole half day a week. The course itself is very practical. It is purely shooting, first on the ground, and then in the air at various kinds of targets, still and moving, then at still targets when you move, and finally at moving targets while moving yourself.

It is worthy of notice that out of thirty odd students enrolled in the school, there are four boys from Detroit—Louis Bredin, Sandy Wetherbee, Kenneth Matheson, and myself. Louis Bredin is Adjutant of the American Contingent.

We have had several indignation meetings here in regard to the whereabouts of other Detroit men, and the ears of many of the bomb-proofers at Washington, Paris, and other dangerous localities must have burned.

We see and hear nothing but guns and aeroplanes all our waking hours.

I am getting along with my work all right, and am in the best of health.

Your loving son,

William.

A. E. F., France,
May 7, 1918.

Dear Father—

My very pleasant stay here is just about concluded, and I have nearly finished the course. This completes my instruction as a chasse pilot. All that remains now is to wait for orders, and orders, we understand, will come when machines are forthcoming. What type of a machine, or when we will get them, or where we will go, there is no telling, but don't worry—there is no need of anxiety for some time yet.

Owing to the good work done last week, we have had Saturday afternoon and Sunday off. It was a great relief to change the atmosphere and permit yourself to relax in a comfortable hotel. In the dining room you see a wonderful conglomeration of uniforms—bright coloured Portuguese, Italian, French, a few Russians and dull khaki Americans. They are full of enthusiasm, doing their final work here. All are boys between the ages of eighteen and twenty-five. Away from camp, they are a jolly lot of friends, saluting and shaking hands all the time, but on the field, there is a great deal of rivalry. The scores at shooting, and the expertness in flying are watched jealously. I am proud to say that the Americans have broken the records here, and their work is favourably spoken of on all hands. The American mechanics, too, have caught on to the foreign motors, especially the rotary Rhone motor. I have used

FONTINALIS

it almost entirely.

During our short stay at Arcachon we could not get in enough baths; so in the afternoon, when out sailing and well away from land, we took a dip in the ocean. We quickly discovered that we were rushing the season, and hurried back to Madam Foulon's, who was kind enough to give us some hot cocoa made with water, but we had to produce our military bread tickets before we could get a slice of *pain grille*. This regulation has been in force since the first of May. Butter is also *defendu*, but we have discovered that an American officer with a little poor French and a good deal of flattery *peut obtenir du beurre*.

Sunday was a lovely day, and all the resorters were out in their glory. The beach was a swarming mass of children and nurses. It amazed me to see how long some of the more sedate and elderly French could occupy a bench on the Pier without moving or apparently thinking. Aside from some food regulations, there was nothing to suggest war times. We learned of an attractive little inn where we might drive for lunch, and we engaged a couple of Louis XIV hacks and had a fine drive.

The scenery, to me, was like northern Michigan, if you substitute the ocean for Lake Superior. The luncheon was delicious—good enough, we thought, for C. O.'s. We lounged about at the wayside Inn all the afternoon, and I was so contented that I cursed the Hun for getting us into service, and wondered whether it would make much difference to the Aviation Corps or the cause of the Allies if a single flyer like myself should fail to show up for further duty; but this was only a daydream. Our permission expired at midnight, and we returned to the field, and reported promptly on time.

The camp on the lake is beautifully located, but there is a fly, if you are polite enough to call them that, in the amber. French troops occupied our barracks before we did, and what I now know to be awful, is here most abundant. Not being able to sleep and scratch at the same time, I give up trying to sleep until, after rolling and tossing until I am tired, I fall off into a doze regardless of the summer boarders. You would not recognise the soldier whose picture you insisted upon having taken the day before we left New York, swabbed and smeared, as he is, with grease; but, as the French say, "*c'est la guerre*" an excuse for anything.

My next move, at the end of the week, will be to return to Issoudun. I am ready and hope to get flying there. Aeroplanes, however, are still lacking. For the interim, I have had an opportunity to take three jobs, none of which appeals to me. One is apt to be left permanently with it, especially if he makes good. I can be a monitor instructor, tester, or take charge of the acrobatic field. The last is by far the most preferable; but, as I say, if I should take it, I might be tied down indefinitely. I think I can arrange so as to wait until a squadron of Americans is formed, or until I can be detailed with a French or English squadron. *Nous verrons.*

I suppose you have read of the excellent work that some of our boys are doing at the front. One squadron, in making its first patrol over the lines, brought down three Boche planes, a remarkable record. It is all wrong that we have not been given more of a chance.

The last two or three days the fine weather disappeared, and except for a couple of lectures on machine guns and deflection, we have held down the benches in the barracks. This always puts the fellows in a discouraged state of mind. In an aviation camp, it gives one an opportunity to think and talk too much.

The climate has got into me, and I have been troubled with a slight cold. I am shaking it off, however, and remain with love to all.

Your loving son,

William.

An American Aviation Field,
France,
May 9, 1918.

Dear Mr. Russel—

I am enclosing a little snap shot of Bill that I took recently, showing the new leather coat which he bought in Paris. It is about the best looking one I have ever seen. Incidentally, I think it is very good of Bill. He is now at an aerial gunnery school finishing the final step in his *Chasse Pilote* training before going *au front.* He did mighty well in his flying training here, receiving A grade at every field. I never saw anyone so happy as he was at being relieved from his job "running an elevator" as he put it, and at flying again,

I am (and have been for two months) one of a staff of seven instructors at this field. One by one, we go to aerial gunnery schools, and in a short time now, our whole bunch will have completed their training, and we hope we will all go to the big show together. I am trying to arrange things so that we will go with Bill when he goes. Everyone is well, and will be glad when the period of "marking time" is over and we are at last in the midst of things, doing our "darndest."

Maury Hill and Ed, Buford have both been up near the line for some time, but so far have had no actual fighting.

Kindest regards to you and Mrs, Russel,

Yours sincerely,

Harry C. Colburn.

******

Note

On May 11th, 1918, before this letter was received. Lieutenant Colburn was killed in an aeroplane accident. He went up in a new machine without a pupil to try the air, and at a height of about one thousand feet, suddenly went into a tail spin and crashed to the earth.

******

A. E. F., France,
May 13, 1918.

Dear Father—

It has been a long slow training, but at last, I have completed my instruction as a *Chasse Pilote*, which you know was my ambition. One might think that training for aviation would run along narrow lines, but not so with mine. It has practically covered the field of military work. Since a year ago last April 26th, in addition to military drill, handling arms and flying, I have done everything from working with a pick and shovel, cleaning up garbage, waiting on table and the highest type of kitchen service, with here and there sprinkled in much clerical work and a few truck convoys. Not counting these many diversions from regular aviation, I have the satisfaction of knowing that I have received far better and more careful instruction than the majority of French and American pilots who have gone to the front. I do not say the British. Their instruction is not as long nor as safe, but once completed, is most thorough.

The excellent results of their fitting is readily seen. Take my class alone—at Memphis, Ashburn, and in the early days of Rantoul, we had as good instruction as was given in the States because it was before many of the other schools were completed, and it was not necessary to divide the instructors among them. We had more time in the air and fewer accidents, but it seems to me now that the principal benefit of our Curtis training was to give the student a sense of the air. We certainly acquired that, and having it, the remainder of the training with those machines, I will not say, was a waste of time, but was of no great advantage, at least to a *chasse* pilot. Nearly everything they tell you not to do in a Curtis is essential in a Nieuport or Spad. The little monoplanes I have never flown and know nothing about them yet.

But to continue—from Rantoul I went directly to Villa Coubley, where, without doubt, you can find the greatest flyers in the world. Adjutant Chatain, my instructor and my friend, is one of the best of the conservative type. I had perfect confidence every minute the plane was under his control, and so, in my very first flights there, I was able to concentrate my thoughts on the new handling of the stick control and the resulting action and movement of the machine. As a result, I was turned loose in a very short time.

After making sure that I had mastered the stick control on the larger machines, comparing in size to a Curtis, I went step by step to the little high-powered Nieuport, which really requires skill to fly. The type of Nieuport I had was the machine used by the members of the Lafayette Esquadrille before their famous Spad was introduced. I think, at the present time, opinion is slowly swinging back to favor the new model Nieuport. Many people, however, are prejudiced against the rotary motor, and I am inclined to agree with them. A stationary motor seems to me to be preferable, but, although I am a *chasse* pilot, I feel that there is so much to learn that I am not ready to express opinions.

I was at Villa Coubley just long enough to familiarize myself per-fectly with the Nieuport and the stick control, when orders came to go to Issoudun. Here came advanced training, acrobatics, formation flying, and aerial combat. I suppose this is the greatest of all flying fields. They have vast tracts of ground containing many square miles divided into ten fields, and as you progress in your air work, you go from field one to eight. The last two fields are not yet finished. Having completed the course there, you are assigned to certain branches of aviation, according to your flying ability, as you are then considered a finished flyer. If you are a good conservative flyer, and develop a fitness for the work, you are sent to either bombing or artillery observation. If you have a faculty for acrobatics, and in formation flying and com-bat, you are almost certain to go *chasse*.

So far, there have not been many sent to the contact patrol group. At this stage, the split comes, and some go to bombing schools, some to aerial gunnery schools, and the rest to artillery schools. My aspi-ration being for *chasse* work, which I consider the highest type (the pursuit pilots are the knight errants of the air), I had the good fortune to be sent here to the best French aerial gunnery school, where I have had a mighty interesting, and, I think, valuable course. My regret is that I cannot stay here until they are ready for us at the front. They will not permit us to remain, and we will probably be used as clerks for some time until planes are ready. We get all kinds of rumours, but one learns very early in army experience not to put any reliance on them. There is a possibility that we may be sent with a French squadron, and this I am personally hoping for.

Just now, I am an idler in a beautiful summer hotel at Arcachon for two days, sleeping until ten or eleven in the morning, and eating more than enough. The intervals are occupied largely with many hot baths, mostly sulphur, necessary for reasons which I have before explained and otherwise.

It is certainly, for the time being, the best war which I have ever fought in—beautiful weather, beautiful scenery, and beautiful rest. Most of the other boys are on horseback. They said they wanted to take a ride on the ground. I am taking the opportunity, while I am on *terra firma*, to write.

This morning I asked about the fishing, but it was in vain. I am not in the right part of France for trout. Many and oft-times I picture myself sitting by the dam near the hatchery at Fontinalis, or wandering slowly up stream past the pools at the cedar bends below the section house meadows. Here, I have even more beautiful scenery, but somehow it is lacking in the thing which would make it most attractive to me, I think, also, it is the want of the old time companionship and the continual change of scene. Everything is strange here. You are constantly moved from place to place and meet new people. I enjoy new acquaintances, and the people are very kind and courteous to me, but it is not my nature, as you know, to rush in and mix with strangers. I have made many good friends, but really the hardest part of my army experience has been the separation from home and the old familiar faces.

You can do a kind act by sending me another letter of credit. My long sojourn in Paris and advances to the government in connection with the various truck convoys have diminished my funds. At present, the United States owes me about twenty-eight hundred *francs*, for which I have pay vouchers in, but have not yet been able to collect. You see that in addition to personal service, I am doing my bit to support the financial credit of my country. I have been able to shake off the little cold which has been bothering me and now feel very fit.

ISSOUDON, MARCH, 1918
(THE COAT)

Not having heard, I am taking it for granted that all of you are well, and with love to all,

Your loving son,

William.

Aviation Section,
A. E. F., France,
May 15, 1918.

Dear Wain—

It was not due to thoughtlessness, merely lack of time, that I have not written sooner. The last month has been a busy one and a great deal has depended upon it. By this I mean my career as an aviator—whether I should be a bomber, an artillery observer, a reconnaissance driver, or a *chasse* pilot. As I told you, my ambition was to be the latter, and this last short period of my training has determined it. I have passed the course successfully. Your fate lies in your ability in formation flying, acrobatics, and combat work. You may be an excellent flyer, but lacking one of these essentials, your chances are minute for *chasse* work.

The other branches were objectionable to me, and sometimes made me shudder on account of one thing—you are required to carry a passenger, either a bomber or a photographer or observer—and the idea of having another man's life depending continually upon your vigilance and skill has never appealed to me. When you have completed your course in combat flying, which includes straight flying, cross-country work, speed scout work, acrobatics, formation flying, and combat, you are selected, and separated from the rest to go to individual fitting for advanced and final work. I had the good luck to be chosen to prepare for *chasse* work, and was sent to an aerial gunnery school. It is, in effect, a course in air shooting where the target and the gun are in motion, and the thing is to find the proper deflection and hit the mark.

At first, you have ground work; shooting with a revolver, and then with a machine gun, which is fired from the rear of a fast motor boat at targets, stationary and moving in the water. The next step is the air work. As you probably know, the guns on a *chasse* plane are aimed by aiming the machine. You take up in your plane a little paper parachute, about the size of a parasol, which you throw over and dive at as it falls. The balloons are captive, and you make a small circle of the field and dive at them and shoot as you pass. At the end of so many shots, usually five hundred, the balloon is pulled down, and the hits recorded. Next comes the "sleeve," usually the final step of the training.

A linen stocking, about twelve feet long and two feet in diameter, is towed some two hundred feet behind one of the larger machines, and you swoop down in your *chasse* machine and shoot at it. It requires care, but is really fun. If you have the faculty, and are successful in making a good record, this completes your course as a *chasse* pilot. That is where I now am, after practically thirteen months of training in which, aside from flying, I have done everything from peeling potatoes to high class clerical work. It has, however, been a good experience, and one which I would not regret if it were not that it has kept me from the front so long, and taken so much out of such a period of a man's life.

Another thing which has been distasteful to me has been the constant change to new localities, new faces, and new friends. Just now I cannot complain, as I am a resorter in a beautiful summer hotel in one of the most popular French seaside resorts. We have only two or three days, but it is a time for good meals, much sleep, and especially plenty of hot baths. I am sure I will have parted with all my unwelcome attaches after a couple more sulphur washings.

There are plenty of pretty women here—cordial, as in all parts of France, to the American uniform. Talking French seems to come easier in their company.

Sometime, when I get back, if I am spared, and am sitting before your fire, I will have great experiences and lively descriptions of France in war time to give you. It seems incredible that such a short time ago one would never have dreamed of them.

This is the loveliest place I have visited, and Wain, with the environment now about me, it is certainly hard to believe that I am going from here to war to fight and kill.

Magazine story parties all day, and all evening, which are novelties to the American, at least to us small-town folk.

About the future, I know little more than you. I am a finished *chasse pilote*, but there are no *chasse* machines available. I am like a man all dressed up and nowhere to go. Bill Casgrain had the good luck to be sent to the front in the first *chasse* squadron which we sent forward, and I understand he is doing good work.

I think that Smut is over here some place, a sergeant in the Dispatch Corps, but I have not had the good fortune to see him. His last letter was from New York. He has, of course, shown the right spirit,

"Bill" and "Smut" (Ward Smith) at Fontinalis

and has had to undergo some rather unpleasant experiences. Smut is the proper colour, and I hope he will come out all right.

Well, Wain, this is just a line to keep in touch with you. Write me as often as you can, and let me know how you are. I trust everything continues as well as in your last encouraging letter. If there is anything you need or want in Detroit, write father, and I am sure that he will do anything for a friend of mine. He has certainly been wonderful to me since I enlisted, before, and all the time. Best luck in the world to you. Love to your mother.

As ever,

Bill Russel.

To Mr. C. W. Stephens,
Albuquerque, N. M.

Aviation Section,
A. E. F., France,
May 18, 1918.

Dear Father—

My delightful month is over. I have forgotten the hardships and feel as if I had spent the time at the Virginia Hot Springs. The only thing lacking was your companionship and the company of other dear old friends. I felt as if I were a resorter like the other loungers, and was not living on borrowed time. The place was so attractive, so quiet, and far enough from the aerodromes that one soon forgot that he was a flyer, and was content to keep both feet on the ground.

Our course at Cazaux was exceedingly interesting, although the hours were long. There was enough bad weather to permit us to run over to Arcachon quite often. If ever you can say, "I, too, have been in Arcachon," you must have looked up Madame Foulon. She serves delicious meals at a reasonable price, an unusual incident to an American officer. We also had the good fortune to have a commanding officer who was a flyer himself, and understood our point of view. The general attitude of officers who are not flyers is that we are flying lieutenants, something quite different from a lieutenant, and you are treated accordingly. I feel sure the day is near at hand, however, when this will all be done away with, and the aviator and the record which he will make will be appreciated.

I am again at my former station, where I am only waiting, no flying nor any classes. Several offers in the flying line have been suggested, but none has met approval, and I have been able to side-step them.

They are not ready for *chasse* pilots yet (I understand the real reason is that planes are lacking), and so they are sending the men into different branches where they will be occupied, such as artillery observation, monitors, testers, and other like jobs, where you are apt to be kept for the remainder of the war, because on becoming efficient, you are too valuable to let go. Sandy Wetherbee is a monitor, and has warned me against offering my services, so I am merely marking time, waiting for call as a chasse pilot, which I hope and pray will come soon.

On my return here, I was shocked by the news that Harry Colburn was killed the day before. Ever since my enlistment, he has been one of my best and closest friends. We took our medical exams, together, and I have lived with him at Memphis, Ashburn, Rantoul, New York, on the boat, Paris, and Issoudun. I have known him day and night, and he was always true blue. After being with a man in such close companionship for nearly fourteen months, it is a terrible bereavement to be suddenly deprived of him, and my heart is very sad, but *c'est la guerre*.

Although I am right here on the spot, I have been able to obtain few details of his death, as this topic is not much discussed after an accident takes place. He was flying along in a natural position, not performing any acrobatics, when his machine, for no apparent cause, suddenly fell into a *vrille* or tail spin, which he immediately corrected, but it seemed as if he over-controlled, and fell into another on the opposite side. This time, he was too near the ground, and could not regain control, and death came to him simultaneously with the crash. I was a mourner at his funeral, but could not show the grief I felt. I have written his club at Indianapolis that they might inform his family, of which, even in all our intimacy, I never heard him speak.

The heat for the last few days has been intense, and I have been loafing in my room nearly all the time, almost nude, waving off flies with one hand, and writing with the other. I am getting as fat as a balloon, but, as a little overweight may come in very handy on future diet, I am not complaining or dieting.

Not a single letter has come from anyone for over a month. I am sure there must be some letters tucked away, and when it cools off, I will go down and raise a riot at the post-office. They told me that I had been changing my location too often to expect to get any mail.

Our permissions are still being held up at the request of the French government. All travel except that which is necessary in military movement has been stopped. We are told that they will be issuing them again in the near future, and if one comes to me, I will try to visit Mr. Jarves for a day or so. I will have to go where I will be a guest. They say now that the only people who can travel and visit hotels in France are millionaires and American generals.

Thinking of pay reminds me that up to the present, we have not drawn a cent of flying pay. Although Congress turned down General Pershing's recommendation, the quartermasters have not yet been instructed to pay and all refuse. All Americans enthusiastically admire General Pershing, but he has something to learn about aviation.

I venture to say that if he had waited longer and learned what service the Aviation Corps will render in this war, and really appreciated the record and the risks of the air corps, he would never have made his recommendation. The distinction between air work and the service in other branches, great and glorious as they are, is evident to anyone who looks. The aid to the artillery and the contribution to the success and safety of troops afforded by the British Royal Flying Corps in its contact work, for instance, ought to be proof. General Pershing, I am sure, will have a change of mind, just as the rest of the world will, very soon.

As it seems that it will be some time before I can be assigned to *chasse* work in a squadron, I think I will apply for a job as a ferry pilot. This requires one to deliver machines from the ports and from the factory to the front. It is not a highly honourable or courageous job, but it allows you to keep your hand in flying all types of machines, and gives you a great knowledge of the geography and topography of the country, and a fine experience in cross-country flying. It will relieve the tedium of doing nothing. One becomes terribly restless, just sitting, when this awful war is going on, and others are in it and calling for you.

Love to all.

Your loving son,

William.

Aviation Section,
A. E. F., France,
May 25, 1918.

Dear Father—

Yesterday was a holiday for me. With the exception of an hour's flying just to keep my hand in, I spent the remainder of the day reading letters, the first I have received in six weeks. Notice the dates; it looks like a scramble—on May 24, one letter from Christine dated

Spad Pursuit Plane (Avion de Chasse) 220 h.p., Two Vicker's Guns
W.M.R. about to take flight at École de Tir Aérien, Cazaux

December 30, 1917, one from Helen dated April 7, 1918, two from you dated April 6 and April 18, one from Wain dated April 14, one from Weeanne and Mary Louise dated April 22, and one from Captain Reilly dated May 9, which came from another post only fourteen miles away. Several newspapers from Mr. Jarves came on record time. I went to the post-office, filed a complaint, and was told that I ought to be happy to have received such a bunch, but was assured that hereafter, I would be taken care of O. K. I was so much pleased that my kick was very gentle. I had not worried, however, because I feel confident that if anything should go wrong, you or someone else will always resort to a cable to our good friend Mr. Sharp. That is the safest and quickest means of communication.

With the exception of a short flight each day, I am still at leisure, waiting and anxious for orders to proceed to the front. I think, without doubt, we will be sent out with a French squadron, and I am well pleased with the prospect for several reasons. First, it will mean that we will probably have the Spad as our *chasse* machine, something we would not have in an American squadron. Second, we will cross the fines with experienced men. Third, the treatment of the French aviator by the army in general is superior to that of an American. There still remains a certain holding aloof of the Flying Corps in our army. What the aviators will do in the air against the enemy and for the Allies is not appreciated, and those of us who are not at the front seem to be looked upon as gentlemanly loungers. You can rest assured that all this will change when the record is made, and I think long before the end of the war.

Until you hear from me, therefore, know that I am an *embusqué*, resting peacefully at the Third Aviation Instruction Centre, enjoying the privileges of the American Red Cross, a wonderful institution. Its work has been marvellous, and has made life in camp comfortable. Just think of such luxuries as rest rooms, restaurants, shower baths, and ice plants—permanent fixtures of an army camp; then the attractive girls from home working with that organisation. It seems to be a requisite that everyone must be a good dancer, and every Saturday we have a party. On these festivities, the nurses from the hospital at Chateauroux also come over, and we have a regular *soiree* with iced tea and salad for refreshment. It may relieve you to know that we have such good company, and enough diversion to prevent us from getting stale.

Although I am content, except for the constant desire to be with the boys doing my part at the front, all is not happiness about me. The last two weeks have been most distressing. The camp has met its first real period of bad luck. In the last ten days, we have had ten fatalities and several lesser accidents. Death is just as terrible in an army camp as on a playground at home, and in each case, there is some poor fellow whose heart you can see is touched with a deeper gloom than the rest. The loss of Harry Colburn came home to me, and it seemed at the first announcement that it would break me up. He was killed while testing a new machine. Since I parted with Maury, Harry has been my closest companion whenever we were stationed together. It was a tribute to him to see the great number of friends he had made in his short army career.

Under a recent order of the Post Office Department, no packages will be accepted from the States whether with a requisition signed by the receiving officer or not. There is no doubt that under present conditions, this is a proper and necessary order, but the government ought to allow the transportation of cigarettes. They are essential to a soldier's life, especially if we go with the French, where we can get only French cigarettes and tobacco. The weed has degenerated in France.

You asked me about the big gun. It is as mysterious to me as to you. I left Paris three days before it began its fearful work, and so have no first-hand information. What I have heard is from men who have come from Paris. At first, it was supposed the bombs were dropped from a new type of plane which would fly extraordinarily high, but the protecting planes of Paris reached an altitude of twenty-two or twenty-three thousand feet, and at that height, they could see or hear nothing. So it was no aeroplane. Then, it was thought that it must be a gun, and it was up to the aeroplanes to determine where it was. They searched the whereabouts of Paris, but could discover nothing. We have since been told that the gun or guns were located on the lines, and that they have been demolished. Whether or not, they have been silent as far as Paris is concerned for some time.

I had a most encouraging letter from Wain yesterday, and was delighted to hear that he has practically recovered his health.

The one great disturbing thing which is in everybody's mind now is the on-coming offensive, which appears to be even more terrible and gigantic than the last. Each day, however, which intervenes, is an encouragement. Every delay on the part of the Germans is to the advantage of the Allies, and so far, the stops have been numerous. There is anxiety, but we can, and surely must, beat back the Huns, and I think that everyone at heart is optimistic of the result.

The letters from home have been most encouraging. At times, especially in this branch of the service, where we are kept waiting, it seems as if little was being done, but your report of your visit to Washington, and of what Detroit is contributing to the cause assures us that victory is only a matter of time.

I am in the best of health, and when I am not thinking of Harry, in good spirits. Love to all.

Your loving son,

William.

A. E. F., France,
May 27, 1918.

Dear Father—

I am laid up today with a stiff neck, the result of a foolish escapade yesterday. The day was perfectly beautiful, and I thought I would take a little jaunt to cool off after loafing all morning in the hot barracks. I was able to get a swift little flyer, and jumped in with nothing on except my old favourite thin buck-skin coat, the same one I wore at Rantoul, and my goggles. The air was perfect, and I sailed about just as a bird does for the joy of the thing, looking at the beautiful country stretched out below me. When I came down, I thought it was one of the most delightful flights I had ever taken, and there was nothing to change my opinion until I waked up this morning with a neck with no joints in it.

I am, therefore, sticking close to the room today, swathed in a muffler soaked with Sloan's liniment, almost as much to the distress of those about me as to myself. You will remember that horse medicine and its exceedingly penetrating odour. I welcome anything different, however, at this time, when there is nothing to do but wait. I am getting restless. This idleness has continued for nearly two weeks. Tomorrow, we are going over to have photographs taken for the French officers, which makes me think that something will come through soon.

I am enclosing you a newspaper clipping relating the exploits of my old room-mate, Ed. Buford. I parted with him at Cazaux, where he completed his course with me. He was fortunate enough to be assigned immediately to an American Esquadrille. I knew he would make good if his luck continued. Bonne chance must keep company with skill in air fighting.

I was glad to get your note enclosing the letter from Harry Wilson. This is the first I have heard from him since we parted at Hill school.

Dick Blodgett, whom I knew at Williams College, and have also seen quite frequently here, was brought down at the front last week. We are told that if he had not endeavoured to reach the hospital, and landed directly, his life might have been saved. He was wounded in three places, and evidently from loss of blood, fainted and crashed to the ground quite near his objective—another fine fellow who has "gone west."

Tomorrow, there will be no work at the camp and memorial services will be held for the boys who have lost their lives in training at this school. The remainder of the day will be a fete, and the boys of the various squadrons will hold a track meet. The enlisted men are worked mighty hard, and certainly are entitled to a day off. On most of the fields here, the average is about four machines to two mechanics.

This seems to me to be far from an interesting letter, and I have talked about incidents which I usually omit, but it is penned by a soldier with a stiff neck, who is penned in a small space between four walls.

Your loving son,

William.

Hotel Continental, Paris,
June 5, 1918.

Dear Father—

Again I have been returned to civilization—my first sight of Paris since March. There is little change in the city except meatless days now, and the sand-bagging of the finer statuary and monuments has been completed. The same noticeable unconcerned attitude of the Parisians remains, and if it were not that the railroad stations were filled with refugees from the lost territory, all would appear natural and charming. It is a most pathetic sight to see these people, with what little belongings they have left, pushing their tired way, with remarkable spirit and little complaint, to some place of quiet. All this, after four years of suffering the deprivations and horrors of war in their own country. The Red Cross and the Y. M. C. A. are holding out a helping hand in every way. Paris is a beehive for them both.

There is no panic now; the populace merely appear to be annoyed by the uncertainty of the big gun throughout the day, and the Gothas by night. I was misinformed when I wrote you that the big gun had been silenced. I see by the morning papers that it keeps up its mission of terror, but so far, to my good fortune, I have not even heard one of the explosions, and there are several each day.

With the night raids, it is otherwise. Out of my four evenings in Paris, three have been rudely interrupted by the shriekings of the sirens, which, to me, are more nerve-racking than the actual raid. One of them came while I was at the theatre, and it was astonishing to observe the coolness with which the majority of the people took the warning, the larger part of the audience being women and children. At the first *alerte*, announcement is made from the stage, and the performance immediately stops. The music continues, but the lights are dim and the people wander slowly towards the doors and out into the street in a most unconcerned manner. If there is any rush or scramble, it is usually by some person or group who want to get the first call on one of the few taxis which may possibly be found.

During a raid, the taxi driver is in clover, usually sprawled out in the back of his 1900 model. You must go to him with your offerings and beg him to set some unreasonable price for a ride to some place convenient to him as near as may be to your destination. Aside from parting with the fabulous sum demanded, I prefer to walk. This can be done with moderate safety. The principal danger is not so much from the bombs as from the protecting barrage which you can see breaking continually in the sky. In each block, there are several *abris* or caves, which hold from thirty to sixty people, to which you can retreat if the bombs begin to drop too near. The great size of the city of Paris also gives you a certain amount of assurance. The city is plunged in darkness, and it is rather amusing to feel your way along through the black streets to your hotel, and to hear the curious remarks of the passengers in the carriages and taxis crawling by you at a slow pace.

The whole thing is thrilling, and the wonderful city of Paris impresses me more on this second visit than on the former. I have had more time to spend at places that are worthwhile. The people, however, tell me again and again that the Paris of today is not that of the before war time. It makes me wonder what it was like. The streets now are bustling with people, sprinkled with uniforms of every type and colour, and the tea rooms and cafes along the boulevards are filled with pretty faces and dresses. It is a constant picture to look upon the streets bordered with tables occupied by animated people, clad in shades of every colour, blending together in one place and standing out like a kaleidoscope at another.

My work at present is still waiting, and I am afraid the same occupation in the daytime will continue for a while yet. Just enough flying in protecting Paris against night raids to keep our hands in. The remainder of the time we are idle. It is becoming very monotonous, and we are all getting more and more anxious to put our hands into the fire at the front.

In my wanderings here, I ran across Vallie again. He has just returned from Italy, where he was doing ambulance work. He said the fever was slowly increasing, and that malaria was imminent to anyone who stayed there. He resigned from the Red Cross, and had decided to return to America, but we have persuaded him to stay here and go into the French artillery.

More papers and magazines from Mr. Jarves, and another kind invitation to visit him. There is no such thing, however, as a permission in the army today.

I have just had a very interesting talk with Andy King. He has returned from England, where he completed a course in night bombing. He is hoping to be sent out very soon with the French. None of us knows from one minute to the next where he will be. I have met many of my Cornell and other friends about Paris. It is certainly the meeting place of the world.

I feel sure I will write again very soon with news. In the meanwhile, give my love to all. Well.

Your loving son,

William.

U. S. Air Service,
A. E. F., France,
June 25, 1918.

Dear Father—

I am sorry for the long delay between this letter and the last, because I am sure it troubled you, but there is no cause for worry.

My work of late has been most interesting, and not at all monotonous. It has taken me over many parts of France in the unique way of by the air. There are quite a group of us, who have finished training, awaiting machines and the organisation of squadrons. In the meantime, they have assembled us at a camp near Paris, where we can go to the various factories and ports to take delivery of machines as fast as they are finished. These planes are all gathered where we are stationed, and as they call for machines from the front or from other schools, it is our duty to deliver them, obtain a receipt, and return to our station. It is delightful work and of the utmost value to a pilot. Not only do you obtain wonderful experience in cross-country flying and the use of a compass, but you must fly any kind of a machine turned over to you.

So far, I have navigated the following: Biplanes and Monoplanes— Spads, Sopwiths, Sampsons, Nieuports (18, 23 and 28), Caudrons, and Voisins. I have made about fifteen trips ranging in distance from one hundred and fifty to two hundred and fifty miles all over a strange country, and each trip differs in the conditions of atmosphere and landing fields. When we are sent to the front to make delivery there, the machines are fully equipped with fighting apparatus except ammunition. It is a foolish practice, but a non-flying officer, who is the one in command, seems to pay little attention to advice about flying.

One of the boys, Steve Brody, was forced down to the ground with several shots through the wing, and he was fortunate to get away with it as he did. Before the last offensive, we used to stop near Château Thierry for gasoline. This town is now in the hands of the Germans, and some of the aeroplanes we delivered have been taken by them. I have been fortunate enough never to collide with any of the Boches yet, but often, returning on the train, I have seen German planes in the course that I have just completed.

I was much disappointed yesterday in missing out on a trip to London in one of the new Liberty motors. Dick Este, a very good friend of mine, had orders to deliver one to Hendon, England. He wanted a companion to relieve him in the flying. I was the logical man, and it was arranged. Our trip, however, came to grief about an hour later in the test flight, when, in making a landing, he hit a hidden furrow. The wheels stuck, and she rolled over on her back.

I have another sad piece of news to tell. Although you do not know the boy, I have often spoken of him in my letters. Joe Trees, who lived with me in Paris, was killed in London. He was flying a Sopwith-Camel, the trickiest kind of a machine, when it caught fire in the air, and he was burned to death. This is the one horror I have in flying. Joe's father is one of the big men of Pittsburgh and Joe was his only son. He was a fine chap and had everything in the world to live for. It is lamentable to think that the poor fellow came to such a dreadful death in an accident.

You will recall my mentioning a Dutchman named Delange, who came over on the boat with us from America, and claimed to have invented a new telephone. He was the man who promised to do so much through his influence with the Holland Minister for any of us if we should be taken prisoner. I picked up a paper a day or two ago, and lo and behold, the news was published that a German spy had been executed in Paris, whose name was Delange, and who posed as the inventor of a new telephone based on the principle of heat waves. We all suspected this man on the boat, and were on our guard. He stuck close to us, and always joined us in the smoking room and wanted to set up the drinks or play cards and foolishly throw away his money. All the time, however, he was asking too many questions. So you can see that although I have done nothing yet for my country, I have had some experiences.

Saturday Nights and magazines keep coming from Mr. Jarves, who is most thoughtful. Another fine package came from Cousin Catharine Leggat from Folkstone, where, by the way, we expected to land on our flight to London yesterday; also a notice from Brown Brothers of another letter of credit. This traveling about France in these days, even by way of the sky, cannot be done for a song or on an aviator's pay. The notice came, just as your welcome letters do, when wanted most.

My prayer now is that the air service will carry on at the front as gloriously as the land forces. Their work has been wonderful, and the French vie with the British in their praise.

Your loving son,

William.

U. S. Air Service,
A. E. F., France,
July 4, 1918.

Dear Father—

Time rolls on and it makes me almost ashamed to say that we are still doing nothing but wait, but I can assure you that none of the pilots is to blame. One must look higher up and back in the States to locate the cause of the delay. Our spirits run high, and you never saw a more enthusiastic crowd, but we have been moved from place to place, fed with vain promises.

My present *sojourn* at Orly has been comfortable and instructive. It is more or less a booking agency where the old squadrons are replenished as men are needed, and new squadrons formed and sent out. While you are on call, you do night flying in defence of Paris, or act as ferry pilot to deliver machines where they are needed. When flying in the dark, not knowing the conditions beneath or the location

ORLY, JULY, 1918

of the aerodrome, there is always the wonder what to do in case of a forced landing. One is glad to see the lights blaze out and to be safe on earth again. Ferry piloting takes you to the various schools, to the front, and to England.

After each trip, you return to Orly by way of Paris, which gets us there very often, and it is then you are made to feel that you are doing nothing. American pilots are so numerous in Paris that it is causing comment, because they seem to be, and really are, idle; and yet, each day one reads in the papers about the German *avions* flying unmolested over the American sectors. The criticism falls upon us. I hope the time will come when the lavish descriptions printed in the American magazines will come true, and that we will be equipped and permitted to do our share in the air like the British. The Royal Air Force is wonderful. Recently, forty German planes and three observation balloons were brought down; six machines failed to return.

Today is the Fourth of July, and is declared a legal holiday in France. A great many people are marching in parades, each with a little American flag. The automobiles are decorated, the stores are draped, and the air is filled with patriotic leaflets dropped from aeroplanes. It is a real Fourth of July celebration, and probably the beginning of many in France.

Your letter and one from Anne made me glad yesterday—the first from the States in two weeks. The only other mail in the interval was a nice note from Cousin Catherine Leggat and a letter from Ed. Buford. Cousin Catherine tells me to write her for anything I want, and says she has seen several of the young Canadian relatives in London. She spoke of Hendrie Hay, the twins, Ian Hendrie, Willie Leggat and Margaret Hay, who had returned to England because her hospital had been inhumanly demolished by German bombs. I am looking forward to the time when I shall have an opportunity to look up a few unknown relatives in England and Scotland.

Toots Wardell, one of my friends at Memphis, Ashburn and Rantoul, was bringing a machine back from England ten days ago, and has not been heard from since. Rabbit Curry was flying with him over the Channel, and he says that after they reached the Continent, Toots flew directly east, and he was unable to head him off. The correct direction is south. If he made a safe landing, he is probably a prisoner in Germany.

Ed. Buford is one of the very few of us at the front, and has done remarkably well. His letter thrilled me. They have a vacancy just now in their squadron, and he has made request that I be called for replacement. This would suit me beyond words. I know most of the fellows in that squadron. It is the one to which Bill Casgrain was attached. I have done what little I can at this end to bring it about, but have no assurance.

Vallie enlisted with the French artillery the first of July and goes to the school at Fontainbleau next week. I am very much pleased. He has done the right thing.

Until you hear again, you can see me in your mind's eye scouting at night, or flying a machine from somewhere to some place and returning on the train, or idly waiting, only waiting, anxious for the call. With love to all. Well.

Your loving son,

William.

American University
Union of Europe,
Paris, France,
July 10, 1918.

Dear Father—

Still on the waiting list, safe and sound, enjoying an occasional excellent meal in Paris, with a warm bath on a Friday or a Saturday as the impulse moves me. It is necessary, however, that the impulse move on either of these nights. A city ordinance permits hotels to have hot water only twice a week. This change of atmosphere from camp to Paris is all that keeps us from going into a decline. After fifteen months of training and waiting, one is ready to prove his worth and endeavours to show it. Instead, we live upon unfulfilled promises which are depressing to the spirit. Of course, it cannot be helped now, and it will take some time to remedy the situation.

In the interval, we must twirl our fingers and be criticized as idlers by the other branches of the army and civilians, and, in fact, by almost everybody. It is too bad that our program has been so delayed, and that the Boches have been able to go ahead and prepare for us so much the more. It has thrown an extra load on the flying corps of the other Allies. The British Royal Air Forces cannot be given too much praise and glory for what they have accomplished, as well as for what they have taught.

One of your Christmas boxes, containing the cigarettes and knitted articles from the kids, and the book, *Cavalry of the Clouds,* was joyfully received yesterday. That book is an accurate and good story of aviation. It gives you an excellent idea of the way the British have worked aviation into unison with the other branches of the service, of which very little has yet been done by the French or the Germans. The two latter have used their planes for *chasse* work and effective bombing, but have hardly touched contact patrol or the use of the plane in attacks with the infantry.

Then, too, in the box, were the knitted socks of Eleanor's which she asked me to give to Harry Colburn. I will pass them on to another. He was buried long before they came. It adds to my grief that Harry never got his chance at the front. The belated package gave me food for thought. Out of the forty-three of us who sailed from New York in October, not counting those who have been fortunate enough to be called to the front, six have been killed and two crippled for life, and the terrible part of it all is that none of them was able to offer his life in action. Although finished pilots, they got no chance, and the only record is, "Died in Aeroplane Accident."

I am enclosing several snapshots which may amuse you, and which will show you the latest addition to the Russel family—one police dog, "Stupide" by name, aged eight months. The name fits either the dog or the master. One thing is sure, I cannot teach him anything. He has, however, a beautiful face and head, and loves me, and seems to be able to converse fluently in French. He probably thinks I am telling him my name when I call him Stupide. The plane in the photo is the machine which was assigned to me at field number eight, and was for my exclusive use during my stay there. No one could touch it except my three mechanics, and if I broke it or piled it up, I had to stay on the ground until it was repaired.

The tension in Paris has subsided with the prospects so much brighter. For a while—it seemed a long time—it was a city of gloom. The feeling of doubt was universal. Fate might fall either way. Now, it is evident that the critical period, for Paris at any rate, is passed. The British have stood up like a stone wall. The stubborn and persistent fighting of the French Poilu cannot be beaten when it comes to a holding fight. Our land forces, and, I hope, a swarm of planes, too, will be there to give the finishing blow.

My health is A No. 1, as you can judge from the photos—not underfed nor underclothed. Hoping that you are all well and happy,

Your loving son,

William.

Orly, July, 1918

Dear Father—

Eventful things have happened since my last letter. A week ago yesterday I was sitting in the Hotel Crillon with several other boys when an orderly entered and asked for Lieutenant Russel. He told me to report immediately to the commanding officer. My past life flitted quickly through my mind, and I could think of no reason for court-martial or any minor offense which might have come to light.

I parted with the fellows and reported at once to the C. O. My knees stopped knocking when he greeted me very cordially. "Sit down, young man. You are about to enter into the final step of your army career. You will proceed to and join the 95th Squadron. A plane will be ready for you tomorrow evening. In the meantime, lay out your route and pack your baggage, which will follow you by truck."

This was my notification. I was delighted because the boys of this squadron are all familiar. It is the same squadron to which Bill Casgrain and Quentin Roosevelt were attached. I obeyed the orders, and the next evening found me all ready to proceed to my destination. I rose from Paris about six in the evening, and after an hour's flight over very attractive country, arrived at my aerodrome. Here, a cordial welcome awaited me, and I was billeted in a cottage in a small French town with an old French woman. My hospitable greeting was followed by very kindly attention, and I can assure you that I am far more comfortable than you can imagine under the circumstances. At dinner time, I was ushered into another small dwelling, where the flying officers of our squadron dine. At last, I have found a place where flying lieutenants are officers, and their position and safety are regarded.

After dinner, Captain Peterson gave me a short talk and informed me that on the morrow, I would go in a patrol up to the lines where I could become accustomed to the action of the aircraft guns and the bursting of their shells. It was a safe enough trip, and, of course, of the utmost interest, as it gave me the first actual sight, a bird's-eye view of the war-ridden country, in one of the busiest sectors of the fighting at this time.

Father, it is truly terrible beyond description—the once beautiful country ravaged and pitted with shell holes, and the homes of the people who were happy so short a time ago, and the attractive buildings and churches either burning or already levelled to the ground in ruin. Very little has escaped the cruel fire of the large guns and the frightful destruction of a merciless enemy. This was my introduction to actual warfare, and my first impression was one of horror and stupefaction. It was far worse than I had thought, and truly, it seems to me that it is inconceivable to one who does not see it with his own eyes. This finished our work for that day, and the rest of my time was spent in studying the map and learning the lay of the country.

The next day I began work in earnest, and was sent in a patrol for action if necessary. We flew at an altitude of between four and five thousand metres, well back of the German lines, looking for whatever trouble might be found. If any had come, I believe that I would have been of little assistance. Although at a high altitude, and bitterly cold, beads of perspiration broke out all over me. I was safe enough, however, huddled up in the middle of the squadron with experienced men on all sides. My instructions were to witness everything, learn directions, and keep out of a fracas unless it should be absolutely necessary to help others or defend myself—observation, and not fighting. I saw many Boche machines but no fighting. Below me all the time was Hell's fire, actually.

My patrol work has advanced slowly in order that I might have entire confidence in myself and feel at home in my machine. It has really been an interesting adventure under the wise and excellent instructions of our flight commander. But, father, enough of this. I know it does not make you happy, and as yet I have done nothing except to observe and be taught and nursed by other more competent and experienced men. I feel, however, that I am about ready for the Boches now, and want to get at them.

After duty yesterday. Captain Peterson was kind enough to take me to the front with him. He was going to visit his cousin, a captain in the field artillery. This brought me well inside our observation balloons in the zone of the German artillery fire. We were equipped with steel helmets and gas masks, and wended our way into a small cluster of woods, where we found a battery of 75's well concealed. It was pleasant and interesting until we heard the buzzing through the air of the German shells. The captain told us that they had been throwing in gas shells all day, but that their range was poor and the projectiles were falling in another patch of woods some three hundred metres away.

★★★★★★

Major Peterson, Ace, after his return from notable foreign service, was killed in an accidental fall of only about seventy-five feet at Daytona, Fla., March 16, 1919.

★★★★★★

Every two or three minutes, we could hear the hissing of the shells and the explosions, which were not very loud. Now and then, when they came a little too close, the captain would telephone to another battery which would open up in retaliation, and change the direction of their fire. To me, to be continually under such a strain would be too nerve-racking. To him, it was merely the daily routine. It certainly takes iron nerves, and in spite of what some may think to be a greater peril, I prefer the quieter work of an aviator. We spent an hour with the battery, and then drove back to our field. It was all very interesting, but I admit a nerve-shaking afternoon.

The change of attitude on the part of the French is strikingly noticeable. At first, they were enthusiastic beyond all bounds over the Americans. Then there was a long period of waiting without action, and their enthusiasm cooled. At times I thought they almost looked askance at us; but once more their admiration and gratitude are unbounded, and they show it in their demonstrative way. *Vive les Americains, hurra, hurra!* Our infantry and the marines have done such superb work. France is ringing with their praise. They have instilled a new spirit into the Allies.

I left Paris safe and sound, and with the exception of the interruption of the big gun, which pounds continually, it was apparently remote from the seat of war. It was a social gathering place, and the Hotel Crillon was our rendezvous. The last day I was there, VaUie, Sid Cole, Rummy, Bob White, and Doc Pumpelly, our French professor at Cornell, were gathered at one table. It was a joyous meeting, and like old times at college. Although I was glad to get the summons, I was sorry to part from the company. Sid Cole has been in the front line since February.

Well, father, at last I am on the battle line, and can write with my head up, and if spared to join you once more, I can look at you without blushing, I hope. It has been a long time for me to wait, but perhaps I am the better for it, and all is well. Love to everybody.

Your loving son,

William.

95th Aero Squadron,

15 Metre Nieuport Pursuit Plane

First Pursuit Group,
United States Air Service,
France, August 3, 1918.

Dear Father—

Time has changed my career from a life of Parisian leisure to one of strenuous work. It came as a great surprise and also a great pleasure. After a year and a half of training, one is prepared to do his part and yet I lingered on a mere recruit, away from the front, merely guarding Paris in night raids and piloting new aeroplanes across France to the front.

The last three weeks, however, have been real and worthwhile. One retires most willingly each evening long before dark to be prepared for the work of the next day, which may start at 3:30 a. m. or 6, according to the report which comes at midnight. An orderly awakens you an hour beforehand, so that you stand prepared when the machines take off for their mission.

It is a beautiful sight to watch the take-off before a patrol. The eighteen machines stand in two columns with all motors going. When the signal is given, the first machine leaves the ground with the second not fifty yards behind, and then the third, etc. On reaching an altitude of some thousand metres, they fall naturally into a circle, revolving about the field. When the last machine has reached the altitude, the two flight leaders, or three it may be, break away from the circle, and the flights drop into position behind their leaders and start for the lines in a continual climb.

Our work is of different types—all with the main purpose, however, of knocking down enemy machines. We may have low patrols from one thousand five hundred to two thousand five hundred metres, or high from three thousand five hundred to five thousand metres. The latter are by far the safest. You are at an advantage and without the constant worry that someone may fall on you from out of the "sun."

Another job which comes under our routine is to act as protectors to the bombing and reconnaissance machines, which are slow and necessarily have to penetrate a long way into Germany.

A fourth mission on which we are sent is to attack balloons which are some five kilometres behind the lines and are quite low and well-guarded by planes and anti-aircraft guns.

The last and most disagreeable work is "strafing" the infantry in action, trains of camions and troops on the march. This is done from an altitude of only two or three hundred metres, and if you are hit you are too far from your own lines to be able to glide into them. At the beginning of the offensive, this fell to our lot several times, but of late we have been entirely relieved from it, for which we are all thankful. The situation is changed and the artillery guided by the high contact patrols were better able to do the work. It is quite amusing, but one has to take too many chances to derive sufficient pleasure from it.

These various air performances have occupied my days for the past three weeks, and although it is for only four hours a day, it is quite tiring work. The strong wind blows on your face all day, and you are ever on the alert, continually watching like a hawk the move of every machine above, below, and around you, with one eye fixed steadily on the sun, if that is possible. Thus we spend the time; two hours in the morning, and then the accustomed wait for the various machines to return and the tales from each. After luncheon the same thing again in the afternoon.

Well, father, enough of this, except to add that we look out for and see everything in the air and on land, and that the Allies have done remarkable work.

My mail has been coming through very well again. Our treatment is of the best. While we are on the ground, every consideration and privilege is given us. Automobiles and the utmost of liberties. Our quarters and the mess, considering the circumstances, are excellent. We are only expected to be ready with our machines for patrol, carry out the orders of that patrol, and the remainder of the time is our own. This has given us ample opportunity to visit the front several times and wander through the wrecked villages and devastated country. It is horrible. We must exact amends for it.

Am in the best of health. With love to all.

>Your loving son,

>>>William.

Before this last letter was received, the following cablegram came:

>>Cablegram
>>Received at Detroit, August 22, 1918.
>>>Sans Origin. No Date.

Allen F. Edwards,
Detroit, Michigan.
William Russel killed in combat August eleventh. Heartfelt sympathy.

>>>>Lyster.

>>>Grosse Pointe Park, Michigan,

229

August 23, 1918.

Father Darling—

William is dead. Such a brief span of life it seems—such a short hour of duty before he made his sacrifice. While I was crying, it came to me that William was ready; that he gave up his life gladly.

I like to think of him with a quiet peace in his heart, a little peace inviolate in the midst of horror and carnage.

When they give up all thought of self, as we know he did, and live face to face with immortality, they take on some of its glory. Their spirit is of God, and, father, I believe they die gladly, if it will help.

When I heard the message, I said to myself, "Can father bear this burden?" You have lost so much. Then I thought of William answering, "Yes." He had no other ties or affiliations. All his admiration and love was for you. He would have said "Yes" believing in your strength. How we stumble when we come to the lesson of fortitude, but, father, you must not. He has been worthy of you. Now it is your turn. We loved him and he is gone, but we can love him still.

Affectionately,

Anne.

COURVILLE, FRANCE

'E'en as he trod that day to God, so walked he from his birth,
In simpleness and gentleness and honour and clean mirth.

★★★★★★★★★★★★★★★

They made him place at the Banquet Board—the Strong Men ranged
thereby,
Who had done his work and held his peace and had no fear to die.

—Kipling.

LEONAUR

ALSO FROM LEONAUR
AVAILABLE IN SOFTCOVER OR HARDCOVER WITH DUST JACKET

THE FALL OF THE MOGHUL EMPIRE OF HINDUSTAN *by H. G. Keene*—By the beginning of the nineteenth century, as British and Indian armies under Lake and Wellesley dominated the scene, a little over half a century of conflict brought the Moghul Empire to its knees.

LADY SALE'S AFGHANISTAN *by Florentia Sale*—An Indomitable Victorian Lady's Account of the Retreat from Kabul During the First Afghan War.

THE CAMPAIGN OF MAGENTA AND SOLFERINO 1859 *by Harold Carmichael Wylly*—The Decisive Conflict for the Unification of Italy.

FRENCH'S CAVALRY CAMPAIGN *by J. G. Maydon*—A Special Correspondent's View of British Army Mounted Troops During the Boer War.

CAVALRY AT WATERLOO *by Sir Evelyn Wood*—British Mounted Troops During the Campaign of 1815.

THE SUBALTERN *by George Robert Gleig*—The Experiences of an Officer of the 85th Light Infantry During the Peninsular War.

NAPOLEON AT BAY, 1814 *by F. Loraine Petre*—The Campaigns to the Fall of the First Empire.

NAPOLEON AND THE CAMPAIGN OF 1806 *by Colonel Vachée*—The Napoleonic Method of Organisation and Command to the Battles of Jena & Auerstädt.

THE COMPLETE ADVENTURES IN THE CONNAUGHT RANGERS *by William Grattan*—The 88th Regiment during the Napoleonic Wars by a Serving Officer.

BUGLER AND OFFICER OF THE RIFLES *by William Green & Harry Smith*—With the 95th (Rifles) during the Peninsular & Waterloo Campaigns of the Napoleonic Wars.

NAPOLEONIC WAR STORIES *by Sir Arthur Quiller-Couch*—Tales of soldiers, spies, battles & sieges from the Peninsular & Waterloo campaingns.

CAPTAIN OF THE 95TH (RIFLES) *by Jonathan Leach*—An officer of Wellington's sharpshooters during the Peninsular, South of France and Waterloo campaigns of the Napoleonic wars.

RIFLEMAN COSTELLO *by Edward Costello*—The adventures of a soldier of the 95th (Rifles) in the Peninsular & Waterloo Campaigns of the Napoleonic wars.

LEONAUR

ALSO FROM LEONAUR
AVAILABLE IN SOFTCOVER OR HARDCOVER WITH DUST JACKET

OFFICERS & GENTLEMEN *by Peter Hawker & William Graham*—Two Accounts of British Officers During the Peninsula War: Officer of Light Dragoons by Peter Hawker & Campaign in Portugal and Spain by William Graham .

THE WALCHEREN EXPEDITION *by Anonymous*—The Experiences of a British Officer of the 81st Regt. During the Campaign in the Low Countries of 1809.

LADIES OF WATERLOO *by Charlotte A. Eaton, Magdalene de Lancey & Juana Smith*—The Experiences of Three Women During the Campaign of 1815: Waterloo Days by Charlotte A. Eaton, A Week at Waterloo by Magdalene de Lancey & Juana's Story by Juana Smith.

JOURNAL OF AN OFFICER IN THE KING'S GERMAN LEGION *by John Frederick Hering*—Recollections of Campaigning During the Napoleonic Wars.

JOURNAL OF AN ARMY SURGEON IN THE PENINSULAR WAR *by Charles Boutflower*—The Recollections of a British Army Medical Man on Campaign During the Napoleonic Wars.

ON CAMPAIGN WITH MOORE AND WELLINGTON *by Anthony Hamilton*—The Experiences of a Soldier of the 43rd Regiment During the Peninsular War.

THE ROAD TO AUSTERLITZ *by R. G. Burton*—Napoleon's Campaign of 1805.

SOLDIERS OF NAPOLEON *by A. J. Doisy De Villargennes & Arthur Chuquet*—The Experiences of the Men of the French First Empire: Under the Eagles by A. J. Doisy De Villargennes & Voices of 1812 by Arthur Chuquet .

INVASION OF FRANCE, 1814 *by F. W. O. Maycock*—The Final Battles of the Napoleonic First Empire.

LEIPZIG—A CONFLICT OF TITANS *by Frederic Shoberl*—A Personal Experience of the 'Battle of the Nations' During the Napoleonic Wars, October 14th-19th, 1813.

SLASHERS *by Charles Cadell*—The Campaigns of the 28th Regiment of Foot During the Napoleonic Wars by a Serving Officer.

BATTLE IMPERIAL *by Charles William Vane*—The Campaigns in Germany & France for the Defeat of Napoleon 1813-1814.

SWIFT & BOLD *by Gibbes Rigaud*—The 60th Rifles During the Peninsula War.

www.ingramcontent.com/pod-product-compliance
Lightning Source LLC
Chambersburg PA
CBHW032049080426
42733CB00006B/208